Meissen

Bettina Schuster

The Porcelain Museum
of Porzellan-Manufaktur Meissen

Edition Leipzig

Cover:
View into the Exhibition Hall
Monumental Épergne, created by Johann Joachim Kaendler, 1747/48

The terms "Böttger stoneware" and "Meissen porelain" used in this
book do not merely designate materials; they are translations of the
following legally protected trademarks of the Meissen State Porcelain
Manufactory:
Böttgersteinzeug®
Meissener Porzellan®
Meissen®

Bibliographic information published by the Deutsche Nationalbibliothek. The Deutsche Nationalbibliothek listet this publication in
Deutsche Nationalbibliografie; detailed bibliographic data are available in the internet at http://dnb.d-nb.de

English translation:
Timothy J. F. Driver

ISBN: 978-3-361-00627-0

Cover design: Lambert and Lambert, Düsseldorf
Layout and typography: Barbara Gomon, Leipzig
Reproduction: Förster & Borries GmbH, Zwickau
Printed by: Westermann Druck GmbH, Zwickau
Printed in Germany
Printed on non-ageing paper made of cellulose bleached
without chlorine.

CONTENTS

Further information

address:	Staatliche Porzellan-Manufaktur Meissen GmbH
	– Porzellan-Museum –
	Talstraße 9, 01662 Meißen
	Visitors' office phone: +49(0)3521 468-208/700,
	Fax: +49(0)3521 468-204
	museum@meissen.com, www.meissen.com
opening hours:	Monday to Sunday: 9:00 p.m. to 6:00 a.m.
	(1st May to 31st Oct.),
	9:00 a.m. to 5:00 p.m. (1st Nov., to 30th April),
	10:00 a.m. to 4:00 p.m. (31st Dec. to 1st Jan.)
	closed on 24th, 25th and 26th Dec.
	guided tours through the demonstration workshops take
	place every 10 minutes and are possible in 14 foreign lan
	guages; personally guided tours in 9 foreign languages.
	Advance reservation recommended.
entrance fees:	6.00 Euro exhibition hall with special exhibition
	8.50 Euro exhibition hall, special exhibition and demon
	stration workshops, explanation via spatial sound
	children from the age of 6–18: 4.50 Euro
	students, handicapped: 50 percent
	family ticked: 18.50 Euro (2 adults and children up to 18 years)
	groups (more than 19 people) 6.50 Euro apiece
	entrance free: children up to the age of 6, multiple
	disabled (100 percent) with assistant
gastronomy:	"Café Meissen"
	Monday to Sunday: 9:00 a.m. to 6 00 p.m.
	"Restaurant Meissen" daily open from: 11:00 a.m.
	phone: +49(0)3521-486-730, fax +49(0)3521-409-240
	email: info@gastronomie-meissen.com
	www.gastronomie-meissen.com
	"Café Meissen" and "Restaurant Meissen" are accessible
	irrespective of museum visit.
	Dishes are served on Meissen Porcelain.

The Porcelain Museum

"Meissen Porcelain®" – words with a welter of associations. They conjure up smoothness, intricacy, elegance and grace, but also the preciousness of reflective and festive hours spent at tastefully laid tables. Generations before us have been susceptible to the fascination of Meissen Porcelain® and it has retained its seductive appeal to the present day – as witnessed by the thousands who pour into Europe's "Capital of Porcelain" each year to find that the high art of porcelain making continues to be practised as beautifully and perfectly as ever. Meissen treasures are amongst the most sought-after in the world. And nowhere can they be marvelled at in such copious numbers as at the Porcelain Manufactory's own museum in Meißen. Amazement is expressed in all languages and in the hushed, reverent tones befitting a cathedral. Measured the pace, intense the beholding; enquiring minds will not hurry past such heritage. A snapshot for the family album is taken in front of the banquet table. People stand in disbelief before a huge sumptuous vase; it was shown at the 1893 International Exhibition in Chicago – but how was it got there? The State Porcelain Manufactory museum sets out, "en bloc" as it were, the artistic lines of development linking all epochs in which use has been made of the "crossed swords" in cobalt-blue whilst also detailing the great precision involved in making "white gold". We invite you to indulge yourself!

Ask the Manufactory's craftworkers, or "porcelainists" as they tend to be known, what is so special about the porcelain they manufacture and they will proudly refer to the pure tradition underpinning the way it is made, which is bound up in the history of Saxony and, of course, in the close relations that exist with the material and its origins. So precious is the material, so hard and so resilient, that Meissen Porcelain® is often passed down from generation to generation. Its reputation and aura of exclusiveness are effectively perpetuated in this way. And yet each age has its own tastes, repeatedly giving rise to the new in a contemporary guise. If it is occasionally asked whether Meissen Porcelain® is still modern, then the answer is simply: yes, Meissen Porcelain® is always modern — though never modish — indeed, it is timeless.

The "Crossed Swords" in the "Blue Onion" pattern-style

9

Demonstration Workshops

How Meissen Porcelain® takes shape

Before touring the Exhibition Hall it is well worth visiting the Demonstration Workshops. Anyone who has been shown the meticulous crafting that goes into Meissen Porcelain® sees the splendour of three centuries on display through different eyes. Even though Meissen®'s unique standing has long been proven by dint of the spectacular discovery of European hard porcelain and the latter's triumphal march through history, it is still worthwhile, over and over again, explicitly drawing attention to its technical and formal credentials. Visitors to our Demonstration Workshops very soon grasp the extraordinary detail with which forms three-dimensionally interpenetrate, the brilliance of the colours used and the astute artistic fashioning of patterns.

The production of Meissen Porcelain® can be experienced in four selected areas. Doubtless there are some who secretly wonder whether everything is really as it is shown to be and who would prefer to watch painters and designers at their actual places of work. This was possible on occasions in the 19th century but proved to be such a nuisance for the artistic staff that a separate area had to be set up for the ever increasing numbers of public visitors. Nowadays, the Manufactory affords the general public glimpses into its internal workings during Open Days held twice a year. The first model workshop was installed in a small building in the Manufactory's inner courtyard on the occasion of its 250th anniversary in 1960. With visitors numbering over 200,000 a year it was soon bursting at the seams, however, and a new Demonstration Workshop was set up in 1972 on the ground floor of the Exhibition Hall. From then on it was possible to accommodate no fewer than 100,000 extra patrons a year. In 1995, the Manufactory decided to further extend its Demonstration Workshop during a complex revamp of the Exhibition Hall, thus adapting it to the greater requirements of the present. Demonstration Workshop I has been available to the public in its present form since Easter 1996. A new building erected in 2005 has given visitors the choice between Demonstration Workshops I and II.

In Demonstration Workshop I, everything worth knowing is conveyed in condensed form at ten-minute intervals by recorded commentary. Tapes can be produced in the most diverse foreign languages. The numerous tour groups, in particular, experience a set routine of limited duration as a rule. Visitors to Demonstration Workshop II, which opens from April to October, are given personal guided tours and have an opportunity to go over detailed issues in face-to-face conversation. By way of introduction, a film provides information on the history of the Manufactory, the raw materials used and the manufacturing technology adopted.

Thrower/modeller

The thrower/modeller acquaints visitors with the production of a hollow vessel (cup with moulding), using a potter's wheel and negative plaster mould, as well as with the shaping of part of a figurine using a squeezing mould. Their principal tool is a kick or potter's wheel that is still foot-operated today. First, porcelain paste is thrown to produce a rudimentary form known as a "slug", which may be either "hollow" or "solid". The thrower in the Demonstration Workshop produces a "hollow slug" while operating the potter's wheel. Using their fingers, they carefully work the paste with the aid of water and draw it upwards. The porcelain slip that forms on the outside is removed with a metal implement. The thrower then cuts the slug off from the extruded column and sets it to one side for the time being. The slug has to be turned into a plaster mould − in five sections in the example shown − that bears the external shape of the cup in reverse, complete with moulding, on the inside.

The thrower now inserts the slug into the plaster mould, uses a small damp sponge to press the porcelain paste up against the wall of the mould and finally cuts the excess paste away from the mould with the aid of a special hand tool. The cup thrown thus acquires the correct shape inside as well as the prescribed body thickness. It is left in the plaster mould for a further 30 minutes or so, during which the plaster absorbs so much water from the porcelain paste that it shrinks and can be easily removed. A base is thrown in the same manner and a suitable handle pressed. All parts are then cleaned, joined with "slip", the name given to liquid porcelain paste, and gone over again. The outcome is to be seen in a showcase behind the thrower's workbench. Once it has dried in the air, the piece undergoes initial "biscuit firing" at 950°C, whereafter it is accorded the Manufactory's "crossed swords" mark in cobalt blue prior to being glazed and, finally, subjected to a second "glost" firing at over 1,400°C. A glance at the cups in the showcase very clearly reveals the difference in size between biscuit-fired and fully-fired glazed

Thrower/modeller

items — amounting to approx. 16 per cent. Following glost firing, therefore, the material is invariably one sixth smaller than at the outset. The original-size models nevertheless live on in the negative plaster moulds, so can be reproduced at random.

Figurines are made as followed: since it is not possible to cast them as complete entities, the original clay models are cut up and negative plaster moulds of each section produced. The porcelain paste is inserted into these plaster moulds, known as squeezing moulds, whereupon the two multiply subdivided halves of the mould are vigorously pressed together. After 30 minutes or so the sections can be removed and subjected to the next stage in the process.

Repairers

In the workshop in which the "repairing" of figurines is demonstrated, those present witness how the damp, as yet unfired sections are meticulously gone over and composed into a single figurine. The use of the term "to repair" in this seemingly incongruous way is unique to the world of porcelain and little is known as to why it was originally adopted.

The principal activities of a repairer at the Meissen Porcelain Manufactory include using special modelling tools to bring out the three-dimensional qualities of a figurine's sections as they emerge from their moulds, removing the "seams" created during casting and reinstating the surface modelling and structure inevitably impaired in the process. This involves accentuating three-dimensional shapes and details such as the fall of folds, hands, faces and special stylistic effects. The various work steps take account of the signature, formal vocabulary and style of the model's creator, all of which have to be mastered within a framework of an extraordinary wealth and diversity of models, thus making exacting qualitative demands upon the repairer.

Once treated, the various sections are, to repeat, joined using liquid porcelain pastes or "slip" to form a single porcelain entity whose parts need to be of like consistency and to fit each other perfectly so as to avoid cracking. The success of these operations is predicated upon contact surfaces being thoroughly keyed and the right slip for the paste being used. How lasting these connections are is greatly dependent on pressure being applied absolutely evenly when joining parts. Besides any complementary modelling, the subsequent overhaul of the composed figure also involves attaching freely modelled attributes such as flowers, plants and trailing creepers. Flat plaster moulds of which a selection are to be found at the repairer's workbench serve as a means of manufacturing the most diverse of flat appliqués such as petals and leaves. Flowers in full relief have to be freely modelled as a rule. The flower's centre and petals are "made in the hand" and fitted together, the flower then being attached as an ornament to the relevant piece with the aid of slip.

When a porcelain figure is reproduced, it is necessary for authenticity's sake to pay heed to functional and aesthetic features in particular. The repairer has recourse to a model to this end. The discerning use and proper handling of kiln furniture such as setters, props and struts both within and external to the figurine has a crucial bearing on how successful firing is where items with complex statics are concerned. The reproduction of porcelain figures accordingly entails an interaction between artisanry and engineering routines and processes.

Once porcelains have dried, they are biscuit-fired, then glazed and "glost" fired, with shrinkage of around 16 per cent occurring here, too. Figurines and groups are subsequently decorated with overglaze colours in the embellishing department and then fired a third time at 900°C.

Figure porcelains make up some 15 per cent of the Manufactory's overall range. Hunting, dancing, wine growing, the lives of exotic peoples, animals domestic and exotic, Saxon mining scenes, trades and crafts and topics ecclesiastical, mythological, allegorical, anecdotal and abstract — the repertoire covers everything from miniature chess sets to large-format sculptures.

It is not only to demonstrate its sense of tradition that the Manufactory continues to champion manual design today – this is the only sure way of guaranteeing its much-celebrated individuality in future, too. No machine would be able to deliver such formal detail.

Repairer

Underglaze painter

Underglaze painting

Here, decoration is applied to the porcelain following initial firing at 950°C. The colours used need to be able to withstand temperatures in excess of 1,400°C during subsequent glost firing. As a result, there are few colours that are suitable for underglaze painting. Surely the most familiar underglaze colour to come from the Meissen Manufactory is one that has been in use since the 1720s, cobalt blue. It is used in the first instance to create Meissen's world-famous "Blue Onion" pattern. "Blue Onion" is a fixed pattern whose design constituents are arranged in a set way on any given item, with the painter using outline templates as a means of dividing up the area to be painted. The pattern's outlines are cut into these templates, which are made of metal foil. A little ground charcoal is sprinkled through the template placed over the biscuit-fired object, causing the pattern's salient contours to appear. This does away with the chore of dividing up the area to be painted. All underglaze designs are dishwasher-safe.

Painting on the actual pattern using a variety of brushes and the cobalt colour mixed with water plus a painting medium calls for the steadiest of hands, since the aqueous paint immediately and irreversibly seeps into the porous, biscuit-fired porcelain body. Thus every brush stroke has to be spot on. Despite the pattern being predefined, the delightful variations so typical of hand-painted work are nevertheless apparent. Once painted, the pattern on the object is a diffuse dark grey. When the piece is then dipped in glaze, the porous porcelain absorbs the liquid glaze and the white layer of glaze that forms conceals the entire design. For demonstration purposes this has only been half completed, enabling the pattern to be seen beneath the layer of glaze. It is glost firing that causes the glaze to become translucent and the colour to become a sparkling blue. The decoration is protected beneath the transparent glaze. Initially grey, the cobalt takes on its chromatic brilliance through firing.

The cobalt blue mark has been painted by hand beneath the glaze of every piece made at the Manufactory since 1722. The glaze actually protects the famous "crossed swords" against manipulation, as the mark is an important means of determining when any item of Meissen porcelain was manufactured. In the case of the "Blue Onion" pattern, the "crossed swords" have additionally been incorporated into a bamboo stem forming part of the design since 1888, a measure adopted to put paid to an increasing tendency at the time to fake the famous pattern. There are now 50 or so companies worldwide producing variations of Blue Onion based on the Meissen model, but it is only in the Meissen Manufactory that the hand-painted original is made. The "Full Green Vineleaf Garland" or "Vineleaf" pattern produced since 1817 is fashioned in much the same way. Once painting and glazing have been completed, there follow 36 hours of glost firing in gas-fired bogie kilns. The individual work steps and production stages can be seen in specimens exhibited.

Overglaze painting

Forming the point of departure for overglaze painting are the fired, still-white porcelains upon whose glazed surface the decoration is painted and which then undergo decoration firing at around 900°C. Overglaze patterns are great in number and variety, including floral, oriental, wildlife, ornithological, figurative, hunting, landscape and fruit designs as well as the aforementioned embellishment of sculptured porcelains. Every type of pattern has its own subdivisions and special features, not all of which can be set out here. Use is made of metal oxide paints made to ancient formulae in the company's own laboratory and exclusively at the disposal of painters from the Manufactory. The colour palette embraces over 10,000 formulae and is hence virtually infinite. Turpentine oil is knifed into the paints so they can be applied. Painting is done with either a brush or a steel nib depending on the type of pattern involved. Corrections can be made to overglaze work prior to firing.

The painter generally only has one colour on their palette at a time and completes all the detail that is in that colour and so on until the entire motif has been produced. The first phase of decoration — the "application" or "drawing" of the pattern — is thus concluded. In the second work phase, all the subtle detail, shading and contrast is again painted on colour by colour until the design has been fully produced. In a large number of patterns, however, the colours have to be mixed on the palette, two typical cases in point being landscape and hunting scenes. Colours may alter considerably during firing, a fact painters need to be aware and take account of. Luminescent Meissen Purple, for instance, is matt brown prior to firing.

Overglaze painting concludes the tour of the Demonstration Workshop.

As already mentioned, even more detailed information on and insights into the manufacture of Meissen Porcelain® can be obtained at our Open Days and by members of our

"Friends of Meissen Porcelain®" Club. You can even try your own hand at Painting and Creativity Seminars held by the Manufactory. Anyone who has been able to experience the marvellous metamorphosis in Meissen® from formless lump of damp paste to gleaming white porcelain object will be united in believing: Meissen Porcelain® is not expensive but valuable and is therefore worth its price!

The architectural history of the Exhibition Hall

The centuries only appear to have passed Meißen by without a trace. Oblivious to the passage of time, Albrechtsburg Castle looms imperiously over the Elbe. The last surviving witness to the Manufactory's formation on 6 June 1710, it divulges few of the secrets from the earliest years of porcelain manufacture. The news that Europe at last had its own porcelain spread to royal courts everywhere like wildfire! It is at the Albrechtsburg that Johann Joachim Kaendler and Gregorius Höroldt originated their famous forms and colours for porcelain. Hence, the Meissen Manufactory, which amidst great chagrin was forced to vacate the fine structure in the second half of the 19th century, was inseparably linked with the castle and the city. Still today, long since the age of microchips and computers, a hint of the Middle Ages pervades the city's courtyards and twisting lanes. Its ambience, which German Romantics such as Ludwig Richter and Karl Spitzweg depict as an idyll, shapes the locals and may well have actually spawned the "porcelainists". Meißen and Meissen® are two sides of the same coin. Anyone hearing or reading the name of the city immediately thinks of Meissen Porcelain®, for nothing has ever done as much to make Meißen familiar as its famous porcelain. The two ways of writing the name will accompany the reader throughout this publication, notably because the terms Meissen Porcelain® and Meissen® are registered trademarks. Up to the present day, the Manufactory has remained something of an island and any traveller visiting it leaves feeling as much a discoverer as Marco Polo.

The goals of this voyage of discovery are to be found in the Exhibition Hall, the building and annexe erected on the Manufactory's present production site in the Triebisch Valley between 1912 and 1916. At the topping-out ceremony on 6 August 1913, Senior Mining Counsellor Dr Julius Heintze (1874–1948), director at the time, summed up its various functions in the following words: "It is designed to simplify the selection process for purchasers, offer collectors an overview of the finest and loveliest items from the Manufactory and, no less negligibly, serve as a source of learning for artists at the Manufactory ..."[1] This sentiment has lost none of its cogency and thus, although the new complex now goes by the name of Porcelain Museum, what is set out below does not exclusively relate to that sphere. The old "Exhibition Hall" title was discarded owing to the increasingly international nature of our patrons; those from abroad tend to find the old name a little misleading.

The Exhibition Hall was inaugurated on 6 January 1916 – during wartime. The Saxon King and his retinue came to visit the following day. Max Adolf Pfeiffer showed him round the firing houses and workshops and, to crown the tour, acquainted him with the newly built Exhibition Hall. The monarch was impressed, possibly even more so by the gentleman who had shown him around than by the actual premises. Shortly before Frederick Augustus III abdicated in 1918, at any rate, he did the Manufactory a great service by appointing Mr Pfeiffer as the youngest director in its history on 1 November 1918.

The Exhibition Hall initially served as a place for storing specimens for sale and production but evolved with time into a high-profile centre for culture and education. There have been painful interludes, though. In the aftermath of World War II, the collection was taken to what was then the Soviet Union. The precious works did not return until 1959, albeit in time for access to the museum to be granted to the public once again in 1960, on the occasion of the Manufactory's 250th anniversary.

The Exhibition Hall displays but a fraction of the vast museum inventory, which comprises over 20,000 porcelains in all. It is the only museum in the world to exhaustively document Meissen porcelain art from its invention to the contemporary age taking in all stylistic periods. Admittedly, it is only possible to exhibit around 3,000 items from this repertoire at any one time and hence the nature of the show is subject to mild fluctuations. Nonetheless, nowhere else in the world is such a wealth of Meissen Porcelain® to be seen. It can of course occur that precisely the item you are looking for is missing from the display owing to its perhaps having gone on tour abroad or to its being used as a model for a fresh casting by one of our staff. It is, in any case, beyond the means of this little book to cover every single item, its aim being to point up focus area and trends.

During the GDR years, renovation work was confined on financial grounds to the interior of the period building, making it a matter of great urgency that it underwent a root-and-branch makeover in 1992. Only thereafter was it able to fully regain its incomparable visual appeal. Conversely, the structure was soon unable to cope with the growing numbers of visitors pouring in, upwards of 400,000 a year. An asymmetrical annexe was added to turn the Exhibition Hall into a fully-fledged Porcelain Museum that, with its spacious foyer, a café and a restaurant plus all the requisite service areas, meets the most modern of requirements. Congresses and special exhibitions can, for instance, now be held in the state-of-the-art building, which is typically 21st century in this respect too. The new Porcelain Museum, therefore, is a highlight for the city and the region.

Adorning the new building's outside façade is a mural made up of individual panels on which the artist Sabine Wachs narrates the history of Meissen Porcelain® using historical fragments of script and exemplary porcelains. The outcome is like a book lying open for the visitor to read and get an idea of what awaits them within. The combination of porcelain and concrete is utterly new, by the way. The photo-concrete used is the fruit of a young, innovative technology and the Manufactory is again proving to be a mould-breaker when it comes to opening up new up-to-the-minute areas of application for porcelain. Seven out of a total of 18 vertical sections (symbolising pages in a book) have been produced in porcelain and eleven in concrete. This contrast potentiates the effect the porcelain has of enriching the face of the building whilst also allowing it to harmoniously blend in with the structure. Motifs from the porcelain are carried over onto the concrete, thus further heightening the overall impact. In the restaurant and café, proof is to be had that coffee drunk out of a Meissen cup or food eaten off a Meissen plate really does taste better. But let us now turn to the pleasures associated with the history of Meissen Porcelain®.

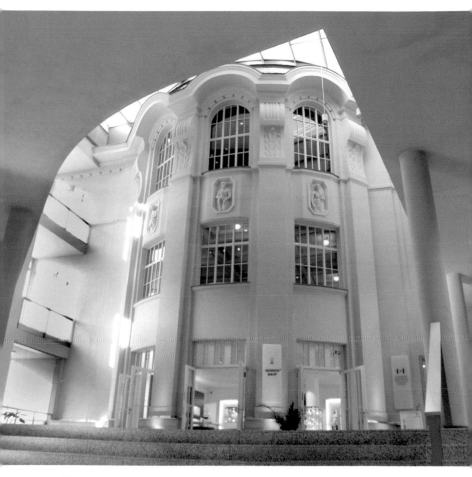

Foyer, crossing to the "Exhibition Hall" and to the Porcelain Shop

Wall plates made of Meissen porcelain and concrete at the outside façade of the museum of the Meissen Porcelain Manufactory, draft: Sabine Wachs

Porcelain Museum

Items in the historical Exhibition Hall are arranged chrono-logically, starting with red stoneware and ending with modern studio porcelains. There are selected pieces in between representing every golden age, every salient stylistic direc-

View into the Exhibition Hall classified as a historical monument;
the architecture shows clear attributes of Art Nouveau, in the background
the ceiling painted by August Achtenhagen (1865–1938)

tion or influence and every major artistic personality that ever worked in or for Meissen®. Visitors to the Museum embark on a journey through centuries of porcelain history in general and Meissen Porcelain® in particular.

The neo-Classicist banqueting hall with its twin flights of stairs impresses concert lovers over and over again just as much as it does visitors to the Museum. With its large banqueting table, graced by a different tableware service each year, it provides a select setting for the many events held at the Manufactory. At the topping-out ceremony for the Exhibition Hall, the building's architect, Mr Schlosser, had voiced the wish that, "once completed, it may fulfil its purpose for centuries to come and help extend the Manufactory's fame and standing far beyond the borders of Saxony ..."[2], something that has indeed come to transpire. But we're getting ahead of ourselves. Here, first, is how it all began.

The "crossed swords" in cobalt blue (first floor tour)

Information on what must be the oldest and most famous trademark in the world is to be found right at the beginning of the tour. It was not long after its formation in 1710 before the fledgling Manufactory had to put up with efforts by others to crack the secret of making porcelain. Despite the first manufacturing premises in Albrechtsburg Castle being seemingly secure and few of those employed having been apprised of the secret involved, already by 1719 fugitive arcanist Samuel Stölzel (1685–1737) had smuggled the secret to Vienna, where he also started up a manufactory. The existence of such competition made it ever more pressing for Meissen® to mark its products in such a distinctive way that they could not be imitated or faked. It was for this reason that, on 8 November 1722, Manufactory Inspector Johann Melchior Steinbrück (1673–1723) proposed identifying every item that left the Manufactory by means of the crossed swords from the Electoral Saxon coat of arms, a very early example of "corporate design", if not the first in the world. Use had initially been made of diverse other symbols such as the initials of Augustus the Strong, the letters A R intertwined or K PM for Royal Porcelain Manufactory before general recourse was had to painting the "crossed swords" in cobalt blue by hand since 1731 – beneath the glaze.

Introduction of the mark coincided with the commencement of production at the Manufactory under trade agreements extending as far as Turkey. In some periods of development, notably under certain directors, additions such as stars, arcs, dots etc. were used. These were at no time of such import, however, that they could have affected the essence of the mark. One exception concerns jasper porcelain (red stoneware), which is stamped with the word "Böttgersteinzeug®" plus the crossed swords. All entries in the Table of Trademarks enjoy legal protection throughout the world and are still used by the Manufactory today. The exact dating of items is a quite separate science that should be left to the relevant experts.

Attempts to fake Meissen Porcelain® are becoming increasingly brazen. But it is not just the Manufactory that faces such trademark piracy. Owners of traditional company names and trademarks the world over lose billions every year. The market for counterfeit goods is growing, the trade

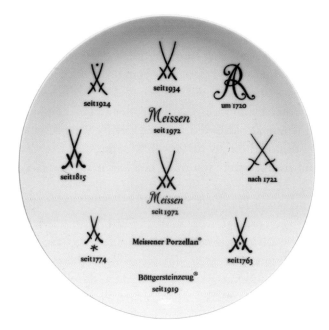

Wall plate with a selection of trademarks from the Meissen Porcelain Manufactory

in copied goods flourishing. Of this, too, proof is to be had at the Museum, though also of the fact that it is well and truly impossible to copy Meissen Porcelain®. In the end, the fakers are done for by levels of quality, knowledge and skills that have been amassed for just on three hundred years.

An inestimable invention

When Johann Friedrich Böttger (1682–1719), an apothecary's apprentice, discovered the secret of making porcelain in 1708, the Chinese had already been producing this finest ceramic ware for over a thousand years. He died in 1719 aged just thirty-seven years, emaciated and racked by illness, with little inkling of how famous he was to become. His life and work have not always been shown in a particularly favourable light. Who was he? Inquisitive scientist and unflagging researcher, all-round genius even, obsessive alchemist or charlatan? Genetically contaminated by his father and grandfather – the one a mintmaster, the other a goldsmith – he tried to make inroads into the secrets of alchemy while still an apprentice. The spectacular experiments he conducted in Berlin startled even esteemed scientists and – having reputedly learned how to make gold – made hurriedly for Saxony in order to flee the Prussian King's henchmen. Once there, however, he fell into the hands of Augustus the Strong (1670–1733), who incarcerated him in Dresden's Jungfernbastei fortification and for a time in Königstein fortress. The belief in the arcanum, the secret of making gold, was still firmly entrenched at many European courts of the time. Böttger's early reputation as an alchemist drew on the assumption that he could turn molten metal into gold by adding a mysterious elixir. But his tests remained unsuccessful.

By now, porcelain from China was all the rage at the royal courts of Europe. The currency of the "white gold" rose in leaps and bounds, "for the lovelier its colours, intricacy, sheen and inherent translucence, the greater the value and appreciation it deserves ..."[3] At the urging and with the sup-

Johann Friedrich Böttger. Bust, Böttger stoneware, by Erich Hösel, 1927 (after a gypsoplast by Franz Andreas Weger, 1810)

port of the scholar Ehrenfried Walther von Tschirnhaus (1651–1708) at any rate, Böttger experimented with manufacturing this equally precious material and is credited with having invented, first, red stoneware, now officially known as Böttgersteinzeug®, in the autumn of 1707 and, a year later, white porcelain. The actual part played by Tschirnhaus has yet to be clarified in every respect. He had already conducted numerous mineral studies and knew the fundamental combination of substances required to create porcelain to the much-admired Chinese model, but had evidently failed to bring the matter to a conclusion. According to Dr Hannes Walter, Director of the Manufactory since 1990, however, his contribution is indisputable and without his input porcelain would probably not have been invented. Tschirnhaus is considered one of the most outstanding German mathematicians and physicists of the 17th century and it was he who first steered Böttger towards ceramics experiments. In this respect, however, mention ought also to be made of the Freiberg smelters whom Mine Supervisor Pabst von Ohain had hand-picked for these trials. "They had experience in metallurgy, which was extremely useful when it came to constructing the kiln, as the familiar potters' kilns do not yield the higher temperatures needed to fire porcelain."[4]

The site chosen for the Manufactory's formation was Albrechtsburg Castle. Böttger became the first administrator of the infant Manufactory. But even in this post, he had to be brought under guard from Dresden, where he continued to experiment, to Meißen so he could fulfil his service obligations. Every effort was made to defend the secret of making porcelain, yet early tea cups and Turkish coffee pots presented at the Leipzig Easter Fair in 1710 really set minds racing. The little city of Meißen became a breeding ground for early "industrial espionage" and, bit by bit, porcelain manufactories sprouted up all over Europe, though the Meissen Manufactory remains the cradle of the fine ceramics industry in Europe and justifiably lauds its products as being Europe's first porcelain.

The first heyday in the 18th century

Böttgersteinzeug® and Böttger porcelain

Chinese porcelain had indeed been the inspiration behind efforts to "recreate" porcelain, and yet the "First European porcelain" is an absolutely unrelated invention of completely different composition, as visitors to the Demonstration Workshop can discover. From the outset, Meissen Porcelain® boasted a quality that rivalled that of the oriental ware Augustus the Strong had so avidly collected. In terms of artistic prowess, however, Meissen® is peerless. This prowess comprises two constituents, the lending of form and the adding of ornamentation. Red stoneware, also known as jasper porcelain owing to its being as hard as the semi-precious stone, is the precursor of white porcelain. It can be polished, ground and cut. Its red colouring derives from the iron-bearing soils with which Böttger experimented.

Johann Friedrich Böttger had officially advised the Dresden Court of his having invented red stoneware and white porcelain in 1709. A process of mechanical refinement hitherto applied to the likes of glass and semi-precious stones had for the first time been used on ceramics — a true first. Fine engravings and intricate mouldings livened up the smooth surfaces. The first "chief designer", goldsmith and court jeweller Johann Jacob Irminger (ca. 1635—1724), was to devote himself "both to red 'jasper' receptacles and to the translucent white porcelain" and supply the attendant designs, models, drawings, moulds and templates. He defined the formal character of the Böttger age. Moulded decorative features known as Irminger appliqués were affixed to porcelains in the form of acanthus leaves, mascarons and borders or else freely modelled petals, leaves and fruit.

The Manufactory went through a period of experimentation in its earliest days and it was here that the foundations were laid for its subsequent pre-eminence. We know that only lime porcelain, also known as Böttger porcelain after its inventor, was made under Böttger. The switch from yellowish calcite to the whiter feldspar porcelain did not occur until the 1720s.

Irminger was succeeded by Johann Gottlieb Kirchner (1706—[probably] 1768), who took up the post of modeller on 29 April 1727 with a view to "inventing all manner of porcelain figures and furnishing them with new adornments". Used to producing large sculptures in stone, he found the changeover to a smaller-format material with utterly different properties and very specific shaping requirements to be somewhat fraught – from both an artistic and a technological point of view. Kirchner accordingly left the Manufactory within a year, only to return in June 1730. He joined forces with Johann Joachim Kaendler the next year to develop the monumental animal statuary requested by Augustus the Strong and in the process learned to master both the

Bottle vase and candlestick. Böttger stoneware, 1715, and covered dish with relief pattern. Böttger porcelain with "Irmingerbelägen" (adornments in the style of Irminger), created by Johann Jakob Irminger, around 1710/12

"Lion", created by Johann Gottlieb Kirchner, around 1730

technical and the artistic principles of porcelain. There was still some way to go before ceramic supremacy was attained though.

The China craze and Johann Gregorius Höroldt

In the earliest period the forms and patterns used for Japanese and Chinese porcelains were simply copied. "The Meißen painters were frequently so adept at copying that the provenance of pieces may be doubtful at first glance."[5] Still today, fabled creatures and motifs from oriental mythology adorn countless porcelains in the "Indian" style. "Indian" patterns acquired this attribute due to the objects copied being brought to Europe on merchant ships operated by The East India Company, whose cargoes were commonly dubbed Indian merchandise. These designs speak a symbolic language, one whose meaning may be hard to fathom. Great work has since been done by Dr Hans Sonntag (born 1944), for many years Head of the Exhibition Hall, on deciphering the symbolic content of these early oriental designs. He ably uncovers the fertile yet submerged world of imagery created by the Chinese and Japanese in his richly illustrated volume "Die Botschaft des Drachen".[6]

Johann Gregorius Höroldt (1696–1775) designed his famous chinoiseries, the dream world of an oriental paradise so beloved of 18th century Europeans, by placing Chinese figures clad in bright garments between exotic trees and shrubs as if on a stage. To make the most of Baroque receptacle design and the exquisite material being worked, he varied his compositions with the subtlety of miniatures and framed them with dainty cartouches in consummate trailing scrollwork. Höroldt's principal artistic achievement was to emancipate porcelain painting from its oriental origins and come up with a great many patterns in the European vein. The most crucial assets he bequeathed to the Manufactory, however, were the resplendently beautiful polychrome enamels he developed. Already back in the 1720s he was attempting to create the coloured grounds of Chinese Kangxi-porcelains. The first mention of a yellow ground dates back to 1725, though it was in the 1730s that coloured-ground porcelains really began to come into their own. Particularly popular alongside yellow were various shades of turquoise and purple.

*Parts of a tea service with yellow ground and Höroldt chinoiseries, form:
Johann Joachim Kaendler, around 1735*

The first porcelain services in Europe

For the first time in the history of porcelain, services came
into being as self-standing ensembles and, with them, famous patterns such as "Dragon" (1731) or "Ornate yellow lion
in the Old Style" (1731). The service with the yellow lion is
evidently the earliest dinner service in Meissen Porcelain®.
Vessels bearing this pattern may have been first made as early as 1728. Most extant pieces are now in collections around
the world.

It was very popular at the time to incorporate the owners' coats-of-arms into services. Porcelain was more than a

Pot, cup with saucer and cream jug: "Ornate yellow lion in the Old Style" pattern, form: created by Johann Joachim Kaendler, 1745

mere status symbol for absolutist rulers. Prestigious platters and plates invariably also constituted a good basis for politics. The high and mighty pursued diplomacy and economic links at the dinner table and the respective hosts were judged by their porcelain. A radically new type of vessels in silver, pewter or ceramics had sprung up around 1700 upon the introduction to Europe of the three "pleasure drinks" coffee, tea and cocoa. The handles on cups and pots proved to be very practical as fingers were afforded better protection when holding them. One of the first problems Kaendler encountered upon joining the Manufactory was that there was "not a single serviceable handle" to be found. It was above all he who in the years thereafter revolutionised European table culture.

The Europeanisation of decoration

The practice of basing floral painting on works of graphic art documents just how effectively porcelain painting managed to free itself from its initially all-defining oriental role model. Known as "Dried Flowers" in porcelain painting, renditions from what were very objective, precise engravings of botanical works reveal the same shaded edging as in the prints they were modelled on. From the mid-18th century, the deutsche Blumen style espoused a more realistic and a more European portrayal of nature. Single cut blooms are generally depicted along with insects and small animals. An indication of its sources is given in the Commission Report for 1745, which lists as reference material "the engravings from Weinmann's great botanical works and other similar drawings".[7] There is a distinct acerbity to these designs, whose botanical and zoological species detail suggests scientific rigour and in which even a wilted leaf or a spent bloom serve as desirable decorative elements.

Further graphic inspiration was found in engravings by Maria Sibylla Merian, Johann Jacob Ridinger, Philips Wouwerman, Nicolaes Berchem, François Boucher and others, all viewable at the Collection of Prints and Drawings in Dresden. Then as now, however, the Manufactory also had its own considerable reserves of such material. This has always been used as a source for the hunting scenes and seascapes that are still amongst the most prized miniatures on Meissen Porcelain®.

Parts of a service with "Flower Painting Based on Copper Engravings" pattern, around 1749, form: I-form, created by Johann Joachim Kaendler, around 1749

The "gallant scenes" that had made Antoine Watteau (1684–1721) one of the most popular artists of his century now became the object of a new decorative style for Meissen Porcelain®. The French painter helped pave the way for the stylistic transition from the Baroque to the Rococo. Gallant couples in scenic parkland settings were his chief motif, one he produced with colouristic aplomb in a great many variants. The costumes worn by Watteau's figures became fashionable to wear in real life. His work had a considerable impact on changing ways of life and artistic styles. 1745 saw the first service sporting "Copper-Green Watteau Scenes", produced to mark the marriage of a Saxon princess to Charles II, King of the Two Sicilies. King Augustus III's "porcelain daughter", as he called Marie Amalie Christine, received it as a gift. The tradition of Watteau painting on Meissen actually dates back to 1741, however, when the Manufactory procured several hundred copperplate engravings after paintings by Watteau and Lancret – a treasure jealously guarded ever since, with work in glistening copper-green still forming part of the Meissen Manufactory's specialist repertoire. Not that Meissen's painters simply copy the engravings they work from. Constraints of space and the need to establish a compositional balance between the painting and the object it adorns are already sufficient to preclude this. Porcelain painting after Watteau is an artistic achievement in its own right that has thrown up an endless wealth of new ideas over the years. Polychrome Watteau paintings do exist, but the use made by Meissen artists of copper green – that prize constituent in the Höroldt body of formulae – in a monochrome "camaieu style" subtly offset by the colouring of faces and hands is unsurpassable. Watteau painting took over as the most significant tableware pattern once the craze for China ebbed away at the Manufactory.

The form of tableware initially preferred for this pattern was "Gotzkowsky Relief". Johann Ernst Gotzkowsky was a merchant from Berlin with whom the Manufactory traded at the time. The relief design bearing his name dates back to 1741. The Marseilles Design was later deemed more suitable. All in all, at any rate, the trend now was increasingly to decorate utility ware in bas-relief, which is modelled into the mould in reverse, as shown on a cup in the Demonstration Workshop. An index of dinner plates from 1790 lists a total of 82 different relief patterns, some with baffling names that now cause the mind to boggle.

The famous Blue Onion pattern

Notwithstanding some slight modifications, the design endearingly known as "Blue Onion" has always retained its basic ingredients — exotic flowers and fruits that no one in Europe was once familiar with. There is no evidence, at the same time, of its being directly based on an oriental model. The experts are still at odds as to which floral forms figured in its inception. On the issue of identifying the elements in the pattern, Lutz Miedtank argues: "It should be agreed that the motif in the wells of plates and dishes, also termed 'shakiako', is made up of bamboo, plum blossom, trailing plant, chrysanthemum and peony."[8] In his view, "blue-and-white" painters at the Manufactory were the undisputed originators of "Blue Onion", because that is the name they later gave it.[9] Let us leave such "fruit disputes" to the experts though. Owing to its aesthetic balance and allure, the Blue Onion

Plate with "Marseille" relief, created around 1745, Multicoloured
Watteau-style figure-painting pattern
Plate with "Onion Pattern" (1734/35) from the coffee service
"Neuer Ausschnitt" form: Johann Joachim Kaendler, 1745

pattern created in 1730 has been replicated and faked like no other design, a further indication of its great fascination. The current range of utility ware numbers over 750 articles. Besides tableware and tea and coffee sets, products supplied have also included toilet furniture, writing utensils, vases, candlesticks and candelabras, culinary items, doll house tableware, tankards and pitchers, petroleum lamps and even flower pots. In keeping with tradition, the rich stock of receptacles in the "Neuer Ausschnitt" tableware service created by Kaendler in around 1745 is supplied in Blue Onion. The indenting (section) on the rim of the plate comprises five long arcs and five shorter ones, which was new at the time, thus the "new" in the name.

46

Sacred statuary

The form of porcelains steadily grew in importance from 1730 and, for 40 years, modelling in Meissen® was the domain of Johann Joachim Kaendler (1706−1775). A series of figures of saints took shape in the 1730s and 1740s alongside groups of worldly subjects. The religious element nevertheless remained firmly in the background except when expressly ordered. Design trends for sacred statuary at the Meissen Manufactory drew on religious paintings from the 16th and 17th centuries, primarily by Italian, Spanish and to an extent also Flemish masters, as well as on statuary from the Italian Baroque. The predominance of Italian Court Baroque in Meissen's production of ecclesiastical porcelain is due first and foremost to Augustus the Strong's conversion to Catholicism in 1697 as a precondition for being crowned King of Poland. One rather special job placed by the Roman Curia involved modelling all the Apostles individually in as large a format as possible. The 42-centimetre high figurines reveal what a strict formal codex the Vatican enforced as regards posture, gestures and clothing. The large-format work entitled "Apostle Peter with Key" was produced in around 1730 by Gottlieb Kirchner. The emphasis is on impassionedness and defiance, the Apostle's qualities he felt it was most important to portray. Bearing witness to these are his proud posture, his very fluidly rendered garments and his expressive, captivating facial expression. Remarkably, the finest representations of the Holy Mary in Meissen Porcelain® were produced by Kaendler, a Protestant. This is a theme that every generation of Meissen artists has returned to at one time or another.

Apostle Peter with Key, created by Johann Gottlieb Kirchner, around 1730

Chief Modeller Kaendler – porcelain art attains perfection

When Kirchner left the Manufactory in 1733, he was succeeded as Chief Modeller by Kaendler. Augustus the Strong
had himself decreed that the Court Sculptor move from
Dresden to Meißen. Kaendler lived and worked on the castle
hill. He had his workshop on the third floor of Albrechtsburg
Castle, a very short walk from where he lived – from 1740
that is, when he bought a house at Domplatz 8. He worked
tirelessly, remaining loyal to the Manufactory for almost
44 years. The figurines he created are the most sought-after
of any produced in any period. Kaendler modelled his loveliest pieces "with free hands". He occasionally worked together
with other modellers – chief amongst them Peter Reinicke
(1715–1768) and Johann Friedrich Eberlein (1695–1749) – on
forms that have since become standard series in Meissen®.
There was no demarcation. Instead, each of the artists involved did their best in the cause of the finished product. The
charm of models from his era derives from their grace and elegance, their life-affirming light-heartedness. In its choice of
topics, too, Meissen® pointed the way for all European porcelain manufactories. Copies of Kaendler's porcelains were
produced throughout Europe and yet none of them ever attained the style and expressiveness of Kaendler's originals.

The period during which the two "giants" of Meissen Por-
celain®, Höroldt and Kaendler, worked together was by no
means harmonious. The constant striving to be the greatest and to be so first undoubtedly caused the rivals many a
sleepless night and yet it netted the Manufactory an inesti-
mable heritage.

The first service with relief appliqué flowers was designed
in 1735. Kaendler formed a déjeuner with roses and small

ribbons affixed for Princess Wilhelmina of Prussia. In 1739, he authored the Snowball Blossom service and in 1740 the "Forget-Me-Not" service. Its vessels are completely covered in moulded flowers, pressed closely together, that were each separately formed and painted by hand. Trailing leaves and branch-like handles add variety to the floral relief. From that point on, vessels with moulded flowers or, indeed, fruit or vegetables became increasingly popular.

Group of shepherds, created by Johann Joachim Kaendler, 1743

A brief word on the passion for collecting: Augustus the Strong claimed he himself was "sick" for porcelain. These days people everywhere collect shepherdesses in high-heel shoes, cavaliers with haughtily expansive demeanours, impish cherubs, the whole comic masquerade of the Rococo and everything that has come since. Tiny as they may be, the figurines and groups in the showcases emit a sparkle and splendour as of gleaming mirror lights, exude a mercurial poise and a charm

Round covered dish and vase with "Snowball Blossom relief" pattern and relief appliqué flowers, created by Johann Joachim Kaendler, around 1736

that is by turn highly natural and highly artificial — a gathering unable to take itself seriously, that renders life a comedy with its contented friskiness. The series on display in the Exhibition Hall are amongst the most cherished items for collectors.

The Swan Service

As already mentioned, diplomatic conversation of the highest order was conducted at table and hosts were measured by the luxuriousness of their table settings. Hence it was no doubt a strategic move by Count Brühl (1700–1763) when he

Nereide and Glaukos with a dish shell, épergnes from the Swan Service, created by Johann Joachim Kaendler and Johann Friedrich Eberlein, 1737-1741

requested a service in keeping with his status from King Augustus III (son of Augustus the Strong) as payment for his activities as Director of the Manufactory (1733–1739). The Count was First Minister at the Saxon Court. Developing the tableware busied Kaendler and Eberlein for three years. Count Brühl's palace was located on the banks of the Elbe and it was because "Brühl" essentially means marshland that the world-famous "Swan Service", all of whose motifs allude to the mythology of water, came to be. In ancient times water was regarded as one of the four elements alongside fire, earth and air. Flowing water was in a particular sense a symbol of the eternal flow of life. Even vessels are in the shape of swans. We again cite Berling here: "The swans and cherubs, Nereids and Tritons, the dolphins, masks, volutes and cartouches of which such opulent use has been made here – have all been treated in such a splendid, airy and yet forceful way and display such consummate mastery of natural forms and the material used that the Swan Service appears to me to be the most momentous work to have emerged from the Manufactory."[10] The "Swan Service" formed the pinnacle of late-Baroque design. It embraced some 2,000 pieces and must surely be the highest fee Meissen has ever had to pay an administrator. Nowadays, of course, Count Brühl would be considered an excellent marketing strategist, since all the major heads of Europe dined at his table only to return home and laud the skills of the Meissen Manufactory in the highest tones. One such was Sir Charles Hanbury-Williams, English envoy to the Court of Augustus III, who banqueted with Brühl in 1748. "Once I was invited to a table at which up to two hundred people were sat. When the dessert was served, I experienced this as the most wonderful I had ever encountered. I felt as if I were in a garden or had been transported to the opera …"

Frederick II of Prussia was not impressed, however. He passed the following verdict on Count Brühl: "He is the man with the largest collection of porcelain, clocks, clothes and boots there has been this century, and thus he is like those of whom Caesar says: 'They are too well-kempt and fragrant for me to fear them.'"

Animal figures and birds

One of Kaendler's first tasks as a young sculptor at Meissen® was to recreate the world of animals in porcelain as faithfully as possible yet in line with the artistic perceptions of the time. What's so striking about his animal figures are their vitality and an extraordinary momentum that invariably captures the essence of the species, a notable example being the famous "Padua Cock". Kaendler generally conducted studies for his exceptional animal sculptures in zoos, zoological collections and natural history collections of the sort fashionable at courts in the 18th century, though he is likely to have turned his observations into sculptural form "in the field" on occasions. The bird farm at Moritzburg to the north of Dresden was conducive to this, for instance. Aside from a few teething problems, he ably dealt with the technology involved. Only the initiated know that special precautions are required for the usually lanky-legged, long-necked and long-tailed animals to prevent any projecting or free-hanging body parts from drooping during firing. Artists and technicians repeatedly marvel at the skill with which Kaendler managed to turn props, bases and similar firing-related requisites into items equally indispensable from an artistic point of view.

"Padua Cook" (detail) with overglaze painting, created by Johann Joachim Kaendler, 1732

Court life in miniature

Among the items regularly achieving top prices at international auctions are "Splendid Pendules in Meissen"®, clocks featuring elaborate figurative ornamentation, ornate flower appliqués and priceless clockwork mechanisms. Mythologi-

Mantel clock with Chinese motives by Johann Gregorius Höroldt, created by Johann Gottlieb Kirchner, around 1728, casting of 1995/96

cal and allegorical themes reflect the transience of time, frequently alluding to the function of the measurer of time, typically Chronos/Saturn as god of time complete with the familiar hourglass, scythe and skull insignia. Such clocks had little to do with telling the time, however, serving instead as ornamental items and status symbols in magnificent gala rooms or intimate boudoirs. Kaendler and Kirchner used to make them and they were also later completed as workshop jobs, incorporating forms from the Manufactory treasure trove such as shepherd groups or animals that were then trimmed with ornate floral garlands. They are not attributable to a specific author, therefore.

Hunting was a pastime engaged in by all royalty in the 18th century, an aristocratic privilege. The extensive woodlands around Dresden, including the Friedewald woods home to Moritzburg Hunting Lodge, Tharandt Forest and the Dresdner Heide woods, contained rich stocks of wildlife. Augustus the Strong's love of pomp and splendour was also apparent in the context of hunting, as exemplified by the Diana Festival or the Great Water Hunt on the Elbe on 18 September 1719. The large Parforce and Hubertus Hunts were particular social highlights. They have been immortalised on porcelain as "Hunting Reports". An eloquent example of this is the hunting goblet made for Prince-Elector Clemens August of Cologne. As Kaendler records in his work report for 3 July 1741: "Goblet prepared and made for the Illustrious Prince- Elector of Cologne to the drawing desired that is $^3/_4$ ell high and doth contain the following figures portraying the parforce hunt." This event has entered hunting history as the "Stag Hunt on High". We know from the work of Johann Elias Ridinger (1698–1767), probably the best-known animal painter of the time whose work was the source of many successful patterns produced at the Manufactory, that drawings in those days were accompanied by a detailed description of the hunting process. As well as being very artistically accomplished, therefore, the hunting goblet simultaneously records a specific event in hunting history: a chronicle in porcelain.

There was also a boom in children, cherubs and little angels. They are shown playing together, charging about, teasing each other or dreamily observing the mythological, theological or historical proceedings. They serve as decorative allegories for the Baroque and Rococo as well as mythologically and allegorically symbolising the seasons, wine or the senses. One reason Johann Joachim Kaendler became the master of European porcelain was that, thanks to the wise teaching of his father, vicar at Fischbach, he acquired a well-nigh inexhaustible stock of mythological concepts.

His hands also shaped enchanting porcelain creations, mostly mirroring the court society of the day "en miniature". Groups and figurines were no mere ornamental accessories but a fully-fledged part of table decorations. Serving Kaendler as inspiration for these were festivities known as "Wirtschaften" at which cavaliers and their ladies dressed up charmingly as peasants, tradespeople and even beggars. They ended up as small and tidy versions in porcelain in the midst of "showpiece banquets" set up amongst artistic parklands, pavilions and water spectacles. Thus there was subject-matter enough for conversation at table. In 1745, Kaendler created a group of 34 street vendors called the "Paris Criers" and, some time after 1753, joined with Reinicke to refashion them in a smaller sanitised edition. Whereas the original

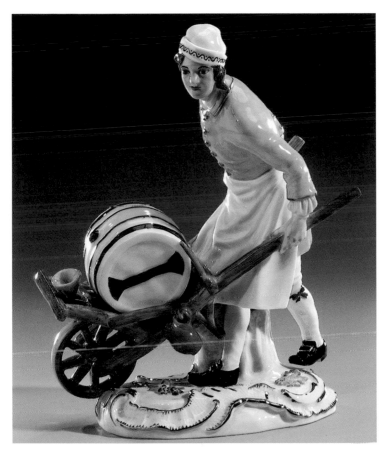

"Paris Criers", *created by Johann Joachim Kaendler, around 1753*

realistically depicts the ordeals of a day's work, the later set focuses more on grace and comic effects. One could claim that Kaendler transformed the "cries" emitted by a strange world of small pedlars and hagglers gathered together under the roofs of Paris and often audible from afar into dignified "criers"— either for reasons of his own or out of consideration for those sections of society who did not wish to be confronted with such hardship and misery. The pedlars were designed after engravings entitled "Etudes prises dans le bas peuple au le Cris de Paris", which Count Caylus produced between 1737 and 1746 and published in several lots. It was probably through the mediation of a Parisian porcelain trader by the name of Huet that the prints came into the Meissen Porcelain Manufactory's possession in 1740.

Military themes may appear to be misplaced on porcelain. They nevertheless crop up time and time again in the Manufactory's history. The Seven Years' War (1756—1763) brought Saxony to the brink of ruin. Frederick II of Prussia was within a whisker of moving the Manufactory to Berlin as "reparations". Luckily, the matter did not go beyond extensive "deliveries" of porcelain. One of the most beautiful tableware services sports the "Prussian Musical Design" — bas-reliefs portraying music and astronomy instruments alternating with military trophies and flowers. Being himself very much blessed by the Muse, the Prussian King also employed the artists of the time. Their figures of soldiers give us a contemporary idea of the weaponry and uniforms in use then.

Mention also needs to be made here of the famous "Monkey Orchestra". Jean Baptiste Guélard produced a series of copperplate engravings after designs by Christophe Huet in 1741/42 whose title translates roughly as "Monkey business or diverse activities in human life as performed by monkeys". The theme was evidently in the air. A more popular theory is often touted about, however, whereby the court orchestra once played so appallingly that its members had to suffer the ignominy of being caricatured in this harsh way. It's an

Figures from the "Monkey Orchestra", created by Johann Joachim Kaendler and Peter Reinicke, 1765

amusing proposition that's got quite a bit going for it, though there is no evidence to back it up. A pronouncement made in 1732 appears to go further towards deciphering Kaendler's moral thrust: "The monkey is the symbol of a useless person ..., because he cannot become a person even when wearing human clothes ..." The first edition of this freakish band with its flamboyant conductor was designed by

Kaendler in 1753. He reworked it in 1765/66 together with modeller Peter Reinicke. The two series have always been amongst the most highly-prized items for collectors. To mark the tercentenary of the birth of Johann Joachim Kaendler, a tambourine player entitled "Le Tambour de Basque" was taken from the aforementioned series of engravings to become the twenty-second monkey in the "Monkey Orchestra" in a special limited campaign. It was shown in this way that the elegance and lightness of Johann Joachim Kaendler's formal vocabulary lives on in the artistic dexterity of today's Manufactory staff.

The famous figurines from the Italian Comedy series – Scaramouche, Harlequin, Columbine and Pulcinello – are set apart by their tragicomic expressions and gestures. The Italian comedy of improvisation, the "Commedia dell'Arte", enjoyed great popularity in 18th-century Europe. Kaendler and Reinicke may well have been inspired to produce their first models in 1743/44 by its bizarre masks and colourful costumes. A further series was produced between 1771 and 1775. A total of 31 figurines and subgroups form part of this series.

The Russian Tsarina Elisabeth I (1709–1762) received the "St. Andrew Service" with Gotzkowsky floral relief as a gift from the Saxon Court in 1744. Besides the cross of the Order of St. Andrew and the double-headed eagle beneath the Tsarist crown, colourful bouquets of flowers and gilt borders adorn the rims of plates and vessels.

Scenes from the height of Saxon silver mining in the 18th century were likewise topical themes and document the various work stages and hierarchical relations obtaining in a Saxon mine, personified by the pit supervisor, mine clerk,

"Columbine" from the "Commedia dell'Arte" series,
created by Johann Joachim Kaendler, around 1764

barrow runner, overman, mine surveyor, breaker and tub carrier. The silver from the Ore Mountains had earlier made Saxony rich. Reminders of this tradition today are the large mine parades that are still held and, yes, the miners in Meissen Porcelain®.

One era comes to a close and another begins

In 1764 the young French sculptor Michel Victor Acier (1736−1799) was appointed to work alongside Kaendler. The artificial world of rose cavaliers died a beautiful death as a new epoch dawned. The art of porcelain changed to reflect prevailing trends. The straight-laced bourgeoisie favoured a less fussy style. Acier was to be the man for a new age, the crossover from Rococo to Classicism. Domestic scenes such as "The Good Mother", "The Good Father" and "Broken Eggs" were now adjudged as being worthy of depiction. The "Great Russian Order" is also from this time. The Russian Court required 40 mythological groups and figures for the collection of Tsarina Catharine II in her summer residence at Oranienbaum. Kaendler and Acier worked together on the job, though Kaendler reserved the largest and most important items for himself.

Acier produced the Motto Children, of which there are 16 in all, to designs by Johann Elias Zeisig (1737−1806), a.k.a. Schenau (Schönau) in 1775. While the little winged cupids do have strong Rococo overtones, the fashioning of the pedestal and stelae is clearly classicist. A shield on the pedestal contains a motto in French, hence the name given to the group. These tiny gods of love busy themselves exclusively with hearts that they either "unfold", "tie up" or "reject". Schenau, who was likewise trained in Paris, supplied the drawings for further figurines and groups while Head of the Painting Department from 1773–1796.

Following Saxony's defeat in the Seven Years' War and the death of Count Brühl, directorship of the Manufactory passed in 1774 to Count Marcolini (1739–1814).

Classicism with its straight, severe forms rediscovered the ideals of antiquity, "noble simplicity and quiet grandeur" as Johann Joachim Winckelmann put it. Clean-lined, oval or rectangular forms with little adornment prevailed. Replicas of ancient sculptures, medallions, statuettes and portrait busts cut a strange picture next to the light-hearted porcelains of the 18th century, and yet the Manufactory managed to negotiate the world of ancient Greek marble with aplomb too. It followed general stylistic trends, dared to embrace change and, by so doing, remained true to itself.

The principal modellers at this time were Johann Karl Schönheit (1730–1805) and Christian Gottfried Jüchtzer (1752–1812). The latter became Chief Modeller in 1794 and, as of 1812, Senior Design Supervisor. He is regarded as having been the main representative of Classicism and, like his assistants, created large numbers of replicas of ancient groups in marble. The demand now was for urn-like receptacles and smooth cylindrical or slightly raked forms with angular handles. Pine cones were used as finials instead of flower buds, while jolly cupids and loving couples on rocaille and organic pedestals were replaced by earnest monuments and busts of heroes on angled baseplates and plinths adorned with laurel wreaths, pendant drapery and meanders. Reality yielded to an abstract ideal, the finest of ceramic materials to a loftier aspiration. A method developed in 1766 was adopted to pro-

"Motto Child": "Las de vaincre je me repose", created
by Michel Victor Acier, 1777

duce what is known as "biscuit" from unglazed porcelain. It
was known full well that this marble or alabaster-like material is difficult to keep clean and yet there was a conviction

"Sealed Love", antiquity figure, created by Johann Gottfried Jüchtzer, 1786

that only through the great degree of detail attainable with biscuit figure castings could the works of antiquity be emulated.

The 19th century and its international expositions

By the time Marcolini's directorship ended in 1813, artistic development at the Manufactory was stagnant and the technical facilities were obsolescent. The company nevertheless rode out the general demise in porcelain making at that time. Whereas formerly significant sites of porcelain production such as Kassel, Fulda, Höchst, Frankental, Kelsterbach, Kloster Veilsdorf, Ludwigsburg and ultimately even the Imperial Manufactory in Vienna were forced to decommission their kilns, Meissen® survived the decades that followed primarily by manufacturing traditional forms and by exporting to England and America.

Biedermeier

Once the wars of liberation against Napoleon had been fought, a brief inward-looking period known as the Biedermeier Age (1818−1848), more a way of life than an artistic style in its own right, was ushered in. Comfort, solidity and functionality were the order of the day for interiors and household implements. Dining rooms with large inviting tables became the focal point of family life. Small services became the fashion: "solitaires" for one person or "tête-à-têtes" for two, as well as a plethora of single cups presented as loving gifts to mark baptisms, birthdays or other family events. Thus arose the interest in collectable cups, which gradually mutated into showpieces so intricately decorated that the actual porcelain disappeared altogether, as the portrait cups for the affluent on display show. People of lesser means were fond of collecting too, however − typically Blue Onion and Vineleaf − one cup at

Cylindrical cups with portraits from members of the Saxon royal dynasty, around 1800

a time, then a cream jug and all the other attendant pieces until, after many years, the service was complete. This form of giving and collecting is well worth considering again today.

The middle classes loved the "Meissen Rose", "Scattered Flowers" and "Full Green Vineleaf Garland" patterns. The latter, often simply known as "Vineleaf", is an elegantly unassuming form of porcelain decoration. It harmonises excellently with the "Swan Handle Service" that came into being in around 1820 to designs by Johann Daniel Schöne (1767—1843). Both form and pattern clearly bear the stylistic traits of classicism. The pattern was authored by Johann Samuel Arnhold (1766 [probably]—1828). His design dates from 1817. The vineleaf motif is nothing unusual in the city of wine. Indeed, mouldings of grapes, vineleaves and trailing vines had been affixed to some of the earliest porcelains. The origins of "Full Green Vineleaf Garland" are related to

Parts of the service "Neuer Ausschnitt" with: "Meissen Rose" pattern,
around 1840

chromatic research by Heinrich Gottlob Kühn (1788–1870).
He addressed himself to the issue of using chromium-oxide
instead of copper as a base for green colours owing to its being highly resistant to temperature as he had established.
Kühn had been appointed Works Inspector in 1814 and later became Manufactory Director. During his directorship,
the task of systematically improving technical processes was
initiated. He also introduced more efficient multiple-storey
kilns that enabled firing capacity to be raised many times
over. The green vineleaf pattern soon became as popular as
Blue Onion.

A certain Georg Friedrich Kersting from Mecklenburg-
Schwerin was introduced to the Dresden public in 1811 at the

Parts of the "Swan Handle Service", created by Johann Daniel Schöne with "Full Green Vineleaf Garland" pattern by Johann Samuel Arnhold, 1817

annually held Art Academy exhibition. In 1818, he was appointed Painting Supervisor at the Manufactory. Though he painted few porcelains himself, he influenced the choice of motifs as well as the quality of drawings and colour combinations. Besides his chromatic sense, what Kersting chiefly brought to bear was his feel for arrangement within a predefined area, for the correlation between form and pattern and for questions as to an item's function, with the result that an increase in artistic quality could soon be felt. Naturalistic floral painting now began to assert itself more and more. It was mainly used on very decorative, showy pieces. It is a type of painting that very much endeavours to capture a flower's natural vitality and complexity.

Parts of a tea service with "Scattered Flowers, Coloured" pattern

"Art is for the people, of what use is it otherwise?" Thus opined Adrian Ludwig Richter (1803–1884), master of late German Romanticism, who painted himself into the hearts and homes of his compatriots as no one else could. He came to Meißen in the spring of 1828, when he was not yet 25 years old, to work as a teacher at the Drawing School. Unfortunately, there is not a single example of his artistic work on show in the Exhibition Hall, as he did no design work for the Manufactory. Mention nevertheless needs to be made of him here because of his bearing on how young professionals at the company developed. The towers and gables of Meißen as portrayed in his book illustrations came to epitomise old-world German cosiness.

From 1828, the Manufactory also made lithophanes or diaphanes, typical products of the Biedermeier. Wafers of a special biscuit porcelain are cast so thinly that, when held up to the light, they can show any work of graphic art in all its nuances due to their being of varying thickness. Paintings and genre pictures replicated in this way were very popular as light shades or window decorations.

A new upturn

1865 saw completion of the move to the new Triebisch Valley premises, for which the Saxon treasury had earmarked 3 million thalers. Within two years, the Manufactory really began to flourish again. Sales revenues for 1871 already amounted to 370,000 thalers. By comparison, the Royal Porcelain Manufactory in Berlin (KPM) earned 160,000 thalers. Six hundred staff had an inhouse repertoire to draw on at the Meissen Manufactory. The elegant classes of England rediscovered the Rococo early in the 19th century. Once customs formalities for the British Isles had been relaxed in 1820, the Meissen Manufactory received so many orders for porcelain in the genre that an entire department was soon given over to the "English taste". Demand was so great that other Manufactories copied Meissen models. Following the rediscovery of the Middle Ages by the Romantic Movement, decoration at the Manufactory likewise went through a neo-Gothic phase. The "style à la cathédrale" took the form of gothic-like pointed arches or tracery. The phenomenon of historicism, in which styles from the past are revived, yielded remarkable examples of consummate

*"Snake Handle Vases", created by Ernst August Leuteritz;
with "Bouquet painting" pattern, 1853*

craftsmanship with which the Manufactory was again able
to excel.

Special mention needs to be made here of Ernst August
Leuteritz. It is he the Manufactory has to thank for its snake

handle vases and the "B and X form", a designation derived from part of the original mould number. Little was he to know that his imposing vases would become the biggest selling items at the Manufactory. In the middle of the 19th century, dense blooms and foliate relief predominated on dishes, plates and cups, often superimposed by a layer of gilding. As well as chromium-oxide green, Kühn had also developed lustrous gold. It was possible to brush on the new gold, which emerged from glost firing "with a vibrant metallic lustre". The extremely arduous process whereby gold applied as a metallic powder is rubbed with an agate tool until lustrous after firing appeared to have been rendered superfluous as a result. The new gilding method produces a matt look on unglazed sections, giving rise to new decorative effects drawing on the interplay of glazed and unglazed elements. Striking gilt mouldings are likewise typical of the "B and X form".

Famous exhibits – second floor tour

Two open staircases lead up to a monumental épergne over which looms a vaulted ceiling with a painting by Professor Achtenhagen from 1915. Johann Joachim Kaendler produced the "Great Temple of Honour" for a banquet held on 5 March 1749. The splendid piece measuring 3.56 metres in height is essentially the centre around which figure groups, single figurines and items of tableware are decoratively arranged. The original casting was probably sold in 1778. The second casting, which has been on display at the Exhibition Hall since 1979, was made between 1920 and 1930. On either side of this "triumphal arch" in porcelain are to be found the most spectacular exhibits produced at the Manufactory for the international expositions of the 19th century. The large candelabra, for instance, is a prototype par excellence for the historicist phase in Meissen porcelain production. Its creator, Carl Hermann Wiedemann (1822–1859), studied Architecture at Dresden under Gottfried Semper and later devoted himself exclusively to decorative art. He also produced the drafts for dishes, cups, vases, jugs and other items. As an architect he was very familiar with all styles. He died at the tender age of 37 and is little remembered today. But, rather than anticipate history, let us proceed with our tour.

At the 1844 Trade Exhibition in Berlin, flower vases with old-style patterns were presented in the new Meissen blue-and-white design together with bulbously curved vases in a traditional form and featuring a new Vineleaf pattern. Accused of subordinating the Manufactory to the whims of fashion, Kühn pleaded economic exigencies. Progressive designs of the kind submitted by Gottfried Semper, architect of the Dresden Opera House, were not in public demand, he went on. During the 1840s, therefore, old styles were produced in a new guise. Conducive to this trend was the change in taste from Late Empire to Neo-Rococo. Openwork baskets were retained from the 18th century, but stands and pedestals were altered so as to attain the dimensions desired as well as being adorned with creations by Kaendler from the Manufactory's stock of figures.

At the 1851 London Exposition, Meissen® for the first time presented a flawlessly fired Semper vase. Only now did progress in firing and glazing techniques make for the desired results. Julius Schnorr von Carolsfeld – professor, painter and Director of Dresden's Art Gallery – had designed panels portraying Bacchanalian scenes in the bas-

"Monumental Épergne", created by Johann Joachim Kacndler, 1747/48

relief of Antiquity for this vase. Meissen® did not attend the second international exposition in 1855 but more than made up for this with its 1862 showing in London. Anyone so inclined had the opportunity to obtain everything from clocks to fireplace panelling in Meissen Porcelain®. Amongst the most celebrated exhibits were vases with painted views of

Dresden, Pillnitz and Meißen, encouraging critics to urge that "views from the Rhine area or Italy be considered for future application" so as to make Meissen® even more internationally competitive. The Manufactory garnered admiration with porcelains in the style of the Italian Renaissance. It additionally presented novel techniques such as enamel and platinum painting, moreover. Six biscuit groups were also shown besides a wealth of services, salvers, trays, candlesticks and figurines.

A great rival emerged as from the mid-19th century in the form of the Imperial Porcelain Manufactory at Sèvres. The French had made quite a stir in 1862 with works incorporating the "pâte-sur-pâte" or "pâte d'application" technique. Actually involved here was a form of decorating known as brushed relief that was already known to the ancient Chinese. White slip is applied to a coloured porcelain ground in varying thicknesses, causing the ground to shine through the relief in nuances and produce a cameo-like effect. Dr Julius Heintze (1846–1931), a chemist who ran the Manufactory laboratory from 1876 to 1895, recreated it for Meissen® in 1878.

The Manufactory again adapted to new developments when, at the third international exposition held in Paris in 1867, it presented works by contemporary artists alongside more traditional material. Tableware sporting the Meissen "Blue Onion" pattern had now become extremely popular. From 1878, porcelains in this style made up a third of all items produced. As an article on the 1873 Vienna Exposition in the Dresdner Presse newspaper put it: "The Meißen factory's output capacity is revealed in the genre of the familiar Rococo groups and what is referred to as Blue Onion, which

Lily of the valley-Déjeuner for the London Exposition 1862,
created by Ernst August Leuteritz, 1861

is applied beneath the glaze, by means of numerous most intricately made samples that are in turn brilliant testimony to the Meißen establishment's proficiency in these special areas of production. Modelled and painted with all the intricacy and flourish of the last century, vases with a virtuosity of full and painstakingly reproduced flowers that is this factory's own. Of particular appeal are vases in 'Limoges', so named owing to the deep blue, uncommonly pure colouring of these vessels brought about by using cobalt as at Limoges, which are also remarkable on account of their tasteful form and decoration, incidentally, notably the figures etched

Wall plate with "Pâte-sur-pâte" technique, probably created by Ernst August Leuteritz, around 1890

in and cut out. This precious genre of artistic work has been most successfully cultivated at Meißen over the past six years."[11] At the 1893 Chicago Exposition, the Manufactory again showed porcelain creations in the historicist style as well as the first tentative examples of Art Nouveau. The most famous client at this time was the Bavarian "fairytale" king Ludwig II. In 1884 and 1885, Meissen® manufactured chandeliers and mirror frames, wash sets, tables, clock cases and door panels for his castles.

Impressionism and art nouveau

Under Kühn's stewardship all technical processes had been brought in line with developments and his inventions profitably utilised. In 1880, Ludwig Sturm became painting department supervisor. He advocated and promoted the copying onto porcelain panels of easel pictures by famous artists, which came into fashion towards the end of the 19th century. This is particularly demanding owing to the fact that, because metal oxide paints only acquire their final chromatic properties upon firing, exactly replicating the material being copied is difficult. Sturm also attempted to reach a healthy compromise between the traditional and the modern, however. Fragrantly painted, almost Impressionist floral designs are typical of this period. With Heintze also developing new high-fire paints, a wide range of colours was now available that specialists such as Eduard Julius Braunsdorf (1841–1922), Otto Eduard Voigt and Theodor Grust adeptly exploited. Braunsdorf's monumental vase with blue roses is certainly one of the most beautiful items on display in the Exhibition Hall. His contemporaries rated him a floral painter of the highest order. Not only do his gouaches and oil paintings exude nobility and elegance, most importantly he found ways of harnessing this quality of execution for porcelain. The light-and-air painting of the French Impressionists was a key source of his creative output.

Achieving the means of decorating vessels and figurines with this palette of underglaze colours led to a completely new form of porcelain design by top art nouveau artists at the turn of the century.

The yearning for technical perfection directed attention towards oriental ceramics once more. Luminously coloured or organically structured glazes that arose as traces of work and the ceramic process were now to make their own aesthetic impact. Successes in this field are similarly associated with the name of Mining Counsellor Heintze. From 1880 he

Vase, created by Ludwig Sturm, with Impressionist floral painting in cobalt blue, by Julius Eduard Braunsdorf, 1896

manufactured a large number of new colour glazes. In 1888, Sprechsaal, periodical for the German ceramics trade, listed as colour shades the Meissen high-fire glazes "light and dark dove-grey, sky blue, dark brown, a soft shimmering seashell red in several shades as well as green and greyish-brown shades". Pieces exist from this period whose only decoration takes the form of colour glazes. The same applies to hairline glazes (crazing).

The art of glazing reached a new pinnacle between 1895 and 1900 when the Manufactory opted to make a soft porcelain on which glazes could be applied more easily and versatilely. There was also an interest in making porcelains with smear and crystal glazes, for which the high temperatures at which Meissen hard-paste porcelain is fired constituted an insuperable obstacle. Great praise was reaped at the 1900 Paris Exposition. The euphoria soon died down at Meissen®, however, as it was too laborious and expensive to produce such pieces and their technical quality was frequently found wanting. The technical development of hire-fire porcelain nonetheless counts as one of the Manufactory's greatest achievements of the period.

The passion for collecting already alluded to in the context of figure groups and cups is also very much alive in the very specialised domain of "Christmas plates". The Meissen Manufactory first issued an edition of this sort in 1910, specifically a plate by Otto Voigt (1870–1949) with a pattern called "Wintery urban architecture in an evening setting". Though seasonal cycles have never held sway, a stately number of such Christmas plates have appeared, all of them incorporating high-fire colours, generally monochrome cobalt blue. Many of them are now very valuable.

The 20th century

Artistic renewal

It became evident after the First World War that the Meissen Manufactory had not lost its freshness. The period was primarily defined by the design work of Erich Hösel (1869–1953) and the painterly input of August Ludwig Achtenhagen (1865–1938). Hösel's "Hun with Horse" won gold at the 1900 Paris Exposition, though the Manufactory had procured the model beforehand and had it cast in porcelain. Hösel applied to work at Meissen® in 1902 and took up a post as Design Supervisor on 1 April 1903. He did much to revitalise the mould inventory and created around 100 models of his own. He was particularly taken by the culture of the North American Indians. In line with this predilection, he produced notable ensembles such as "Bison Hunt" or "Dance of the Medicine Man" for the Manufactory in his first years there. It is not known whether the artist was inspired by the Radebeul-based writer Karl May. Foreign peoples had been popular porcelain motifs back in the 18th century, the Chinese, Malabars and Turks immediately springing to mind. Animal statuary in particular now experienced quite a revival as individual pieces and groups. Hösel's influence caused the Manufactory to regain its leading position in this sphere.

Prominent sculptors and designers with whom it worked delivered seminal creations of which "Lady Playing Bowls" by Berlin sculptor Walter Schott is a case in point. The girl's sense of immersion and her swirling dress are, however, strangely at odds with the period Louis Seize plinth. But these were vestiges that the Manufactory soon discarded. Art nouveau broke radically with all imitation of historical styles.

"Lady Playing Bowls", created by Walther Schott, 1862
"Dance of the Medicine Man", created by Erich Hösel, 1907

Its undular lines were inspired by Nature and the (re)discovery of Oriental art. Following initial hesitation, the new style found expression at Meissen® in a breathtaking output of works that, as well as being products of their age, also reveal a provenance typical of Meissen®. Well over 40 new services were created at the Manufactory in the first three decades of the 20th century, whilst even the Manufactory itself would be stretched to put a number on the new figurative items created during this period. Whatever, it certainly captured the spirit of the age on porcelain in characteristic manner. For most of the 19th century and before, a subtly reflective form of rendition had been preferred. What was so fundamentally new about Impressionism and art nouveau was the concept of interpretative rendition, a purpose to which porcelain is ideally suited.

Great emphasis was placed during this period on the relevance of landscape to art, as is reflected in the frequent use of images of the Meißen area in the work of, for instance, Artur Barth (1878−1926). As is still the case today, many painters were wont to go "landscaping" in their leisure time, meaning they would search the area around Meißen for suitable plants and other motifs with which to enrich their repertoires. The Hentschel children are not far removed from Ludwig Richter either; they are modest, peaceable, soulful − identifiably from this city in other words. Whilst essentially embracing the totality of culture, Meissen Porcelain® nevertheless has a specifically Saxon flavour that is proudly at one with the people here.

It is a period that saw a whole panoply of artists work for Meissen® and help mould its distinctive spirit, amongst them Van de Velde, Riemerschmid, the Hentschel family, Hösel, Grust, Walther, Voigt, Barth, Stein, Marcks, Nick, Eichler, Börner, Niemeyer, Scheurich and Esser. All their various outpourings were rooted in a deep-seated tradition to which they simply lent contemporary expression. The common nature of the porcelain art they produced is indicative of an inner intent and necessity. At the same time, they are as varied as their creators. The service designs of this period mostly involve a thorough-going interpenetration of form and vegetable decor as in the Meissen Crocus and Wing patterns. A non-representational style of decoration was achieved by Henry van de Velde (1836−1957) in his exten-

Parts of service with cobalt blue underglaze painting,
designed by Henry van de Velde, 1903/04

sively linear designs. The underlying demands for material
and function-responsive manufacture made by the Werk-
bund and Bauhaus led to unfussy purpose-driven forms in
which decoration plays a subordinate role, "for the essence
of porcelain is rooted in light. Porcelain imbibes light and
radiates it back out, refracted a thousand times over, as white
light. Hence the white sheen is the selfmost essence it gives
itself. Unfolding this inner light to the full is the goal ..."[12]

The "Pfeiffer Age"

Alongside the production technique brought to perfection during these years and the particularly prodigious output of that generation of artisans, the Manufactory was also blessed with having Max Adolf Pfeiffer (1875–1957), a director with a sense of art, specialist knowledge and leadership qualities who presided over a high point in the Manufactory's history. As he wrote in 1919: "Our Manufactory is one of the few places where the joy of work still flourishes due to a favourable destiny having kept the frenzy at bay that regards earning money as being the be-all and end-all. In order to preserve this most precious of assets, we tolerate no half measures let alone falseness in our work, tolerate no auxiliary resources or procedures that appear to deliver more than they do; rather, we demand quite uncategorically that each piece exceeds what it promises." Elsewhere he adds: "If our work is to gain esteem in the world, this is to be achieved not by pandering to the wishes and views of others but by most lovingly evolving what it is that sets us apart, by consciously reinforcing what is uniquely our own and healthy in our work."[13]

Pfeiffer began his career at the Manufactory in 1913 as Commercial Director, rose to become Works Director in 1918 and, from 1926 to 1933, was Director General. Artistic works were produced during his period of tenure that, whilst being of their time, extended far beyond it. Still today, they are setting benchmarks for design acumen and the aesthetically acceptable in the face of hectic change and that which goes by the name of fashion. Pfeiffer also showed how to go about achieving such artistic quality and establishing an alternative to a tradition crippled by prescriptive forces acting both from within and from without. Freelance artistic work came very much to the fore during this period, for instance, and was instrumental in the recognition and success once again enjoyed by the Manufactory.

Designs that have stood the test of time are, in particular, those by Paul Scheurich (1883−1945) and Max Esser (1845−1943). Scheurich is regarded as being the most important discovery for porcelain statuary in the early 20th century. Over a hundred of his creations have become part and parcel of the Meissen Manufactory repertoire. They tend to be labelled as being art deco, a style from the 1920s, that "golden" decade commonly associated with dances like the Charleston, fashion phenomena like bobbed hair and inventions like the radio, though also with unemployment and inflation. An increasing degree of stylisation informs the porcelains designed at this time. Scheurich usually tried to lend his figurines − some white, some colourfully embellished − an extravagant sweep or exaggerated posture. As a contemporary author said of him, "If Scheurich fills entire sketch books with studies for Meissen porcelain, and … continues drawing in the gallant style of the age, he will actually achieve the epidermis of the 18th century, glaze by means of areas left white, powder by means of a slight shimmer between the beauty-patch stippling of his design tool." His elegant, knavishly slender creatures with their erotic overtones, piquant and coquettish, are the very embodiment of the 1920s in porcelain. The jestful weightlessness and almost choreographic quality of figurines and groups such as those from his "Russian Ballet" put them on a par with Kaendler's work.

On 29 May 1910, the famous ballet troupe led by Sergey Diaghilev put on a production of Mikhail Fokin's "Carnival" ballet pantomime at Berlin's Theater des Westens. The ballet's characters served as models for a group of dancers designed by Paul Scheurich in 1913. His Harlequin figurine is a loving homage to solo dancer Vaclav Nijinsky. With their Commedia dell'Arte costumes and 18th-century elegance, the "Russian Ballet" dancers are as beautiful as anything that has ever been fashioned in porcelain. All of his figurines are somehow not of this world, given up to some floating dreamy abandon. Not long after the Manufactory had argued that it already had enough nakedness on its shelves, its critics were silenced by his Diana. Scheurich also won no end of major international prizes by the way.

Berlin sculptor Max Esser (1885–1943) was the artist who worked most closely with the Manufactory on a freelance basis during the Pfeiffer period. His "Reynard the Fox" table ensemble took shape between 1919 and 1926 after the epic of the same name by Johann Wolfgang von Goethe. It comprises 75 pieces and was one of two major artworks from this period, the other being Börner's war memorial which the Manufactory dedicated to the dead of the First World War. Despite subordinating itself to the white of the porcelain, the colour used enhances the work's decorative effect and three-dimensional quality. Esser's smaller animals have a gripping inner momentum, as splendidly exemplified by his "Otter" of 1931. Esser was superb at rendering the materiality of animal fur on porcelain or Böttgersteinzeug®. He won a grand prix for his "Otter" at the 1937 Paris Exposition. Scheurich, too, won quite a few major international prizes incidentally. Esser also specialised in unconventional chess sets. In line with his penchant for animal statuary, he conceived most of his chess pieces as animals. Indeed, leaving aside the large-scale sculptures produced by Kaendler and Kirchner, the 20th century was the

"Lady with Fan", created by Paul Scheurich, 1930

golden age of animal statuary. Artists who predominantly depicted animals were long dismissed as "hunting painters" or else ignored altogether by art historians. That was set to change now, though. Sculptors of note besides Esser who addressed themselves to this subject include Willi Münch-Khe, August Gaul, Otto Pilz and Erich Hösel.

Of the art nouveau artists who emerged from the Manufactory workshops, mention additionally needs to be made of Konrad Hentschel (1872–1907) and Emil Paul Börner (1888–1970). Börner was one of the most versatile artists from this period. During the many years he worked for Meissen®, from when he joined the Manufactory in 1910 until he assumed overall artistic control, he was active both as a form designer and as a painter. As well as developing new tableware forms, he also devoted himself with great skill to the design of artistic medals and badges. The first playable porcelain bells are also frequently attributed to Börner. On the occasion of Meißen's millennium celebrations they were to be heard intoning the hymn "Grosser Gott, wir loben Dich" from the city's Church of Our Lady.

Mention is already made of the making of "certain bells to be used in a glockenspiel" in Kaendler's work report for January 1732. That set of bells is now in the porcelain collection in the Dresden Zwinger, though the sound it produces is less than perfect. A total of over 50 such sets of bells have now been made at the Manufactory and can be found in cities as far apart as Arita in Japan and Zwickau in Saxony.

Börner's vessel forms are strikingly clean-lined and functional, whilst his decorative work marries chromatic restraint to astonishing expressiveness. As already mentioned, he also designed the panels and, in some cases, monumental figures for the memorial to the victims of the First World War in the Romance Church of St. Nicholas in Meißen, which have now almost sunk into general oblivion unfortunately.

The new (20th) century had been proclaimed as the "century of the child". Attitudes to children and their upbringing had changed thanks to Fröbel and Maria Montessori. Whereas children had hitherto been treated as little adults, it was now realised that their physical and spiritual growth is subject to separate laws. A year before Käthe Kruse appeared with her subsequently famous dolls, Konrad Hentschel, designer and modeller at the Manufactory, painted figures of children that ensured his name would live on, since they came to be known as the Hentschel Children. The series comprises 14 figurines. Hentschel died at the tender

African elephant as candlestick, created by Max Esser, 1924
Child with hat of paper, created by Konrad Hentschel, 1905

age of 35. In his obituary in the Meißner Tageblatt of 14 August 1907, the editor wrote: "I feel I will not be refuted by the circle of his artistic contemporaries if I state that, as a modeller of people, Konrad Hentschel was latterly the most fertile, successful and promising force at the Manufactory. Now that he had been granted greater latitude, he had discovered not only his own style but also the right porcelain style. His delightful, truly refreshing child scenes – which are self-explanatory – are unique of their kind, are Meißen, Saxon, are not simply 'cherubs' in modern dress, and comport themselves just as authentically as the children painted by Ludwig Richter in his prime ..."

One of the artistic personalities who worked for Meissen® at that time was Ernst Barlach (1870–1938). He felt affinities with the late-Gothic woodcarving of his North German home. He turned the vocabulary of this art into a modern, expressive, symbolically condensed form of realism. In no sense, therefore, was he beholden to the heritage of, say, Kaendler or Bustelli. It is initially very hard to imagine his work in porcelain, but Pfeiffer still managed to win his services for the Manufactory. Barlach opted to produce his sculptures in brown stoneware rather than porcelain, however. His works draw their impact from their severe contours, with faces and garments allowing the inner essence of the subject portrayed to become visible by fusing it into a single entity. This effect is most clearly seen in Barlach's "God the Father". As well as being thematically unusual and engrossing, this sculpture is also unparalleled in the manner of its execution. "God the Father" hovers above the Earth as in Barlach's depiction of God the Father in his lithograph cycle entitled "The Transformations of God". Like Barlach,

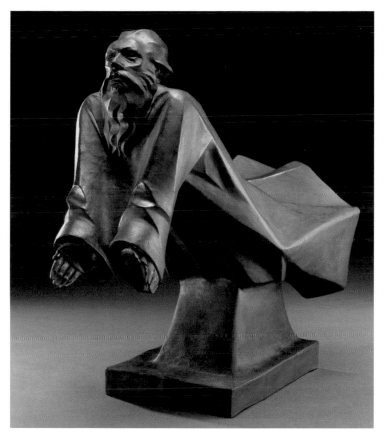

*"God the Father" or "Floating Man", fine stoneware,
created by Ernst Barlach, 1923*

Gerhard Marcks (1889–1981) held Böttgersteinzeug® in
high regard, though he co-designed his "Horseman Candlestick" for white porcelain. "Girl Sleepwalking" was likewise
intended for both materials.

A self-confident generation of artists

The scene immediately after the Second World War was one of desolation despite the Manufactory buildings having escaped largely unscathed. The business was run for a time – until 1949 – as part of the Soviet "Zement" joint-stock company under the Russian Director General Nikotin. Thereafter it was "returned" to the GDR and converted into a "people's own company". Resurrecting its true identity took several years. A technical and artistic new beginning was made certainly no earlier than 1960 that led to a synthesis between awareness of tradition and a contemporary approach. Prior to this there were merely rather ineffectual attempts to use Meissen Porcelainv as everyday tableware and for propaganda purposes. Short-sighted political influence aimed at infusing new artistic creations with the dogmas of socialist realism was rebuffed at the factory gate or else stifled in half-heartedly compliant products that the international market, as ever open for Meissen®, simply ignored.

A trio made up of form designer Ludwig Zepner (born 1931), pattern designer Heinz Werner (born 1928) and sculptural artist Peter Strang (born 1937) came into being some time after 1964 as the nucleus of what was to became the "Artistic Development Collective". They went about giving Meissen® a fresh voice amongst European manufactories in new ways. They were very soon joined by two further pattern designers, Rudi Stolle (1919–1996) and Volkmar Bretschneider (born 1930). The initial period was not easy, but confidence grew in the light of increasing recognition – undoubtedly influenced to no little degree by a new Director, Prof. Karl Petermann (1929–1983). "Petermann demonstrably took this to mean the … integration of duty and choice. With his intensely emotional commitment to the development of new porcelains, which inevitably calls to mind the ambitious approach adopted between 1913 and 1933 by Pfeiffer, he imaginatively succeeded in heightening the two elements by deploying them to the good of each other."[14] Peter Strang left a circensian memorial to the group with a very original parody of himself and his colleagues, a series of magically beautiful, jovial yet somewhat melancholic "Musical Clowns" caricaturing each of the five artists with an ironic glint.

Successful large tableware services, of which "Grosser Ausschnitt" is a shining example, were to the taste of a clientele predominantly resident on the other side of the Iron Curtain. The deeply indented rim that gives the form its German name is common to all receptacles and, in conjunction with

"Musical Clowns" series, created by Peter Strang, 1987/89

*Vegetable dish out of the tableware service "Grosser Ausschnitt",
created by Ludwig Zepner with "Arabian Nights" pattern by Heinz Werner,
in cooperation with Rudi Stolle, 1973/74*

the rhythmic curvature of the scalloping conjures up floral associations. Ludwig Zepner designed the service in 1973, whilst the "pattern designers" came up with over 20 types of decoration for it. The "Arabian Nights" pattern was devised by Heinz Werner in collaboration with Rudi Stolle after motifs and episodes from the collection of oriental tales of the same name. Figurative scenes in the expressionist vein run round the bodies of vessels. Plate forms feature the curtain detail only. In fact, it was Werner who pointed the way for service patterns in general in the second half of the 20th century as well as for the embellishment of figurative Meissen Porcelains®. More than

Cake dish (1973) and teapot (1969) of the "Grosser Ausschnitt" service, created by Ludwig Zepner with "Flower Dance" pattern (after Shakespeare's "A Midsummer Night's Dream") by Heinz Werner, in cooperation with Rudi Stolle, 1969

60 service designs were produced in the fifty years of his activity. Besides "Arabian Nights" it is particularly worth mentioning "A Midsummer Night's Dream", "Hunting Painting" and "Orchid on Branch". The expansion of the Artistic Mural department was largely his doing. In producing studio porcelains, Werner came up with a wealth of richly varied works drawing on trusted subjects that frequently made it straight onto the international market. He also created a number of no less original and multifarious objects on new themes and involving new techniques. As from 1979, Heinz Werner combined his artistic activities for the Manufactory with lecturing on Pattern Design at the College for Industrial Design in Halle. He became a professor in 1981. By lending such profile to porcelain imagery and wall art, Werner founded a whole new tradition at the Manufactory.

The style of Meissen vessel porcelain that held sway in the 40 years to the turn of the millennium bears the hallmark of Ludwig Zepner. He received his academic training in Berlin. He later taught at the institute at which he had gained his own design diploma. In the difficult initial years after 1960, he served as Artistic Head of the Manufactory. Despite having this additional duty, he fashioned an impressive wealth of model porcelains, the first being the "Collective Service" in a "Münchhausen" pattern. Items deserving to be picked out alongside the aforementioned "Grosser Ausschnitt" service complex are the tea service in "Flower Dance" floral relief, the "Japan Ensemble", the "Kumitate" tea service and the "Cone" ensemble featuring his own "Plus-Minus" pattern. Shape is given to this pattern through the principle of motion and countermotion. Its effect is an optical illusion achieved by separating the affixed pattern from its ground.

The design method involved has clear parallels with the constructivist geometrical abstractions of Victor Vasarely, one of the founders of Op Art, and takes some getting used to on Meissen Porcelain®.

Intensive Nature studies formed the basis of Zepner's creativity but were augmented with everything from philosophical observations to a consideration of, variously, the laws of harmonics, the basics of mathematics and overall ontological interactions. He transposed such thinking into robust physicality, dynamic verve and a sensitive formal language. There is much Nature in his forms, much local content, much Saxon Baroque.

Volkmar Bretschneider's career at the Manufactory led fairly straightforwardly through the Drawing School and Painting Department to the Artist Group. He mastered the whole gamut of porcelain painting. Over the years, he developed a very singular signature that, following his involvement in patterns for the large services and embellishing work for figurines

"Cone" ensemble with "Plus-Minus" pattern, created by Ludwig Zepner, 1986

by Peter Strang, notably manifested itself in one-offs. His studio porcelains are marked by mutually repellent qualities such as excitation and calm or aggression and devotion, as he may well be himself. He is the drummer amongst the circus clowns.

"Vase with face of a girl", created by Volkmar Bretschneider, made of enamel colour, 1988, form: Ludwig Zepner, 1989 (unique copy)

He often detaches himself completely from the real world: his creativity expresses itself by turn as something wind-swept, dissipating, diffuse and exploding. He is simultaneously adept at painting impressionist flowers and breathing florid forms of atmospheric airiness onto porcelain.

Rudi Stolle was the eldest member of the Artist Group. He, too, initially worked on devising patterns for the new services. His training as a lithographer was always plain to see. In the 1970s and 1980s, he evolved his own unmistakeable style. Stolle used a pointed brush and sometimes a pen to translate what he saw, experienced and thought onto porcelain. His messages are often fascinatingly structured examples of graphic art encrypted into metaphors, symbols and parables like Babylonian hieroglyphs. The subjects he selected for his extraordinary porcelain paintings were both microcosmic and macrocosmic in origin. His more pictorial compositions exude great decorative appeal along the lines of van Gogh and Vasarely and are primarily to be encountered on large-scale studio porcelains. They now grace many a collection, mostly in Japan, whither several study trips took him.

The first sculptures by Peter Strang were susceptible to a certain academic stiffness. Like his fellow artists, however, he soon hit upon a distinctive formal terminology that had echoes of his role models Scheurich and Esser. Strang also derived inspiration from the theatre, as had great porcelain artists from the past, advancing this tradition of porcelain modelling through contemporary means of expression. The most compelling examples of his "Storm and Stress Years" are "Oberon" and "Titania" taken from "A Midsummer Night's Dream" by William Shakespeare, "Mack the Knife's Wedding" taken from "The Threepenny Opera" by Bertolt Brecht and three figurines from "The Dragon", a comic fairytale by Yevgeny Schwarz. In fact, themes from theatre, variety and the circus arena recur regularly in his creative output. Meeting the gifted actor Armin Mueller-Stahl must also have been a particularly felicitous event for Strang as an artist. In the film "Utz", based on the best-selling book of the same name by Bruce Chatwin, Mueller-Stahl plays an obsessive collector of Meissen porcelain figurines. Strang spent almost a year working on a sculpture of him, a figurine with almost portrait-like traits. The Hollywood star received the first copy of the "Collector" on the occasion of the film's premiere in Dresden.

The figure workshop set up by Strang operates on the principle of the "free build-up" of figures. The practice of freely

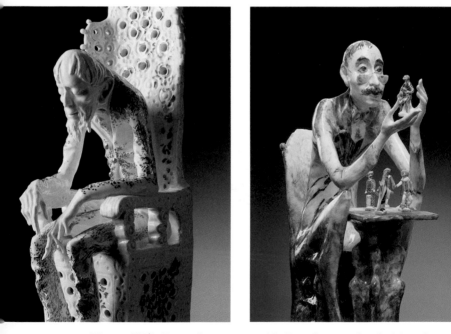

Figure of "The Dragon" group, created by Peter Strang, after the fairy tale having the same name, 1968
"The Collector", created by Peter Strang, 1992/93

modelling the porcelain paste by hand is adopted for contemporary porcelains in particular. It is also possible to combine replicable forms with freely modelled elements. Here, reproducible basic forms such as pedestals or bodies are cast from plaster moulds as usual while all other parts are modelled and attached freely by hand, making each piece truly unique.

Studio porcelain

1982 saw studio porcelains finally put on a comparatively equal footing with the standard range and special series, i.e. with "model porcelains" that can be randomly duplicated and have always been made at the Manufactory. High-quality model porcelain nevertheless remains the core objective. Custom pieces have been produced throughout – as orders from or gifts to monarchs and princes, exhibits for international expositions or because, for whatever reason, they happened to be cast once only. Artists at the Manufactory only began producing one-offs and small series – objets d'art – in specially appointed design departments (studios) very recently at any rate. A new modernism has been induced by such artistic one-offs. The customarily cosy, skittishly high-spirited nature of 18th-century porcelains has made way for something less up-front. Today's work actively provokes discussion and communication, itself a treasured tradition, though the themes have changed.

It is necessary all the while to bear in mind the difficult 1960 beginnings and a social setting in which outlandish Meissen Porcelain® was only tacitly approved – enjoying unlimited freedom to a degree – due to the hard currency it earned and on image grounds. Thus in no way did it stand to reason that the new artistic force would manage to juxtapose a seemingly suffocating tradition with self-sufficient modernity or that innovations could really be forged out of the Manufactory heritage that would become attractive exemplars of the masterful treatment of "white gold". In all of this, Meissen® has remained true to itself — through creative renewal committed to excellence. Strang invariably recites the following metaphor: "The Manufactory is a 300-year-old tree. Its huge bulky trunk is our support leg. A few new leaves are always bursting open up in its crown, meanwhile. The leaves fall, but the trunk of our legacy gets thicker and thicker. The roots have also got to be healthy so the crown can get even broader and house even more crazy colourful birds."

What, along with their beauty and usefulness, makes desirable collectors' items of such individually made porcelains is their rarity — or it always has been at least. Usefulness is actually immaterial where one-offs, ancient or modern, are concerned. As Goethe says, it is a privilege of the beautiful that it does not need to be useful. The use value of studio porcelains, be they wall dishes, vases, boxes or freely configured sculptures, is sometimes questionable and yet, through the agency of beauty, decorative appeal coalesces with rarity to yield an object of value. Such novel exhibits do not always accord with inherited ways of seeing, since they include bold items that are well nigh futuristic in tone. There is a need to constantly experiment with the medium, sound out its limits and in this way ensure the artistic future of Meissen Porcelain®. Art is nevertheless always also predicated upon bread, to paraphrase Director Pfeiffer; it is common to talk of duty and choice. The Manufactory has to live. The Exhibition Hall, therefore, represents both duty and, yes, choice. In pluralism and variety lies its great opportunity.

*Dish, created by Ludwig Zepner, around 1988, with enamel painting
"Fantastic World of Mountains" by Rudi Stolle, 1988 (unique copy)*

German reunification brought further incisions and rupturing, as can be elicited from the porcelains of the time. In
the Manufactory, too, such rupturing stood for new depar-
tures that imparted motion to what had become ossified and
created room for fresh creativity. One particular caesura was
rendered visible through the 1992 "Von Wegen" exhibition
in which representatives of the up-and-coming generation of
artists at the Manufactory made their widely reported debut.

The Meissen Porcelain Manufactory today

Heritage and innovation not mutually exclusive

Meissen® has managed for over a quarter of a millennium to preserve its character and secure an artistic and economic standing. That is in large part due to its craftwork achievements but also to its always having succeeded in harnessing key insights from science and technology without violating the principles of manufactory production. The processes that mould the visual appearance of Meissen Porcelain® remain unaffected by such changes. Quite a few inventions of great significance for pottery are attributable to the Meissen Manufactory. Whenever it has briefly found itself lagging behind in any way, it has invariably caught up again very quickly. This tradition is effectively a mandate and, as already mentioned, technical innovations play an eminently important role in all areas of production that only indirectly impinge upon craft activities. It is possible with their aid to free up creativity and skill in the cause of creating porcelain of great aesthetic value in the spirit of the 21st century. One particularly conspicuous example of this innovative thrust is the design of the façade for the Porcelain Museum.

The Manufactory has also devised a technique for manufacturing wafers of porcelain less than a millimetre thick. They provided the platform for a spectacular venture with "Glashütte original", which involved fitting clocks with faces in Meissen Porcelain®, as well as for cooperation with other suppliers of luxury goods. Karl Lagerfeld, for instance, has already deployed Meissen porcelain wafers as paillettes for festive attire by Chanel Haute Couture. The sphere of jewellery is one in which the Manufactory has been particularly active in developing exclusive products in liaison with outstanding goldsmiths. New areas of application for Meissen Porcelain® include bodies for writing gear by Mont Blanc, ornamental elements on glasses cases or even pages for a first porcelain book.

A stock of operatives with qualifications conducive to preserving the spirit of Meissen Porcelain® has been retained at the Manufactory. These are capable of nurturing the classic range with utter accomplishment as well as adapting it to the modern age in an "acquire-to-possess" spirit. Today's way of life, table manners and home environments are different from those of the 18th and 19th centuries. The Manufactory has heeded this by developing "Classics for Today" that allow random permutations of service components to suit individual aspirations. One example is the "Blue Onion Style" pattern, which pares Blue Onion down to its essence. Further examples of this "lived tradition" are bowls for muesli or receptacles for now de rigueur types of coffee such as latte macchiato or café au lait. The Manufactory is showing with forays of this kind that even its classic range is in tune with younger generations of consumers.

Anchored in tradition as it is, the Meissen Porcelain Manufactory conceives the task of actively nurturing its heritage as also being to lovingly (re-)discover items from its vast history that have been forgotten or lost or, indeed, never existed. A fitting framework for this is provided by the many jubilees with which today's Manufactory staff honour the feats of their magnificent forebears. In recent years, for instance, unique reproductions and special editions have been issued to mark the tercentenary of the births of Höroldt and Kaendler respectively that show how authoritatively the

Manufactory deals with its historical references. We mention the 22nd monkey in our outline of the Monkey Orchestra above. Another striking example is the mustard cruet from the Swan Service, which Kaendler designed in around 1739. No museum in the world has a copy of it today. The Manufactory's archives still had the plaster moulds from Kaendler's time, however, enabling the cruet to be faithfully recreated. Unique showpieces can likewise be reproduced at random in this way, as is the case with the crater vase originally designed by Design Supervisor Ernst August Leuteritz in 1856, which was presented at the 2001 Frankfurt "Ambiente" Fair.

During "Höroldt Year" in 1996, the Manufactory ran an exhibition at Albrechtsburg Castle in Meißen and the Knauf Museum at Iphofen that showed chinoiseries from Höroldt's pattern book plus early designs after engravings by the likes of Ridinger, Watteau or Wouwerman to document the extraordinary breadth and variety of painting in this epoch. Composing patterns to historical models requires a high degree of creativity and skill, as has already been mentioned above. It is to the best of its painters that the Manufactory entrusts such jobs. But for initiatives of this kind to succeed, cooperation between all divisions at the Manufactory is crucial. Laboratory operatives, for instance, have managed to restore the entire palette of lustre colours from light pink to chocolate brown.

Creations for the future

The Manufactory has long since returned to grooming its own artistic young blood whilst at the same time also opening up its doors to noted freelance artists like Astrid Dannegger, Kap-Sun-Hwang, Regina Junge, Peter Makolies, Heidi Manthey, Sonngard Marcks, Astrid and Gerd Lucke, Bärbel Thoelke and Petrus Wandrey, to name but a few. New material is being produced that justifiably bears the "crossed swords" in cobalt blue. Porcelain calls for a form of design that gets a peaceful, pleasurable and intelligent message across. Breeziness and wit are welcome ingredients in this quest. Today's artists — some of them female, unlike in previous centuries — promise to yield advances that will help the Manufactory copperbottom its traditionally leading position. They are in the best sense model pupils of whom their "elders" speak with respect. Their messages in turn are "very much of today", as befits any such handover. Exhibitions on individual artists are frequently held, as are joint shows.

People shape work just as work shapes people. The artists Sabine Wachs, Sylvia Klöde and Gudrun Gaube constitute a correlation that is varied, differentiated and individualised. The Porcelain Manufactory is their common denominator. It is at once their provenance and their umbrella. They are members of a large family of artists going back three centuries. The past is an ongoing challenge as well as a source of pure craftsmanship and internalised affinity with Nature, the foundations upon which they rest. Their differing outlooks nevertheless enable them to create porcelains that are distinctive and unique. Though model porcelain is still the core business, there is an increasing trend towards studio porcelain, exclusive small series and one-offs.

Graduate designer Sabine Wachs (born 1960) has worked on series production and what is known as the studio range

*Parts of the "Wave play" service, created by Sabine Wachs, 2000,
with "Floral Tendril" pattern by Gudrun Gaube*

since 1986. She studied Vessel Design at the College of Industrial Design at Burg Giebichenstein in Halle. Bearing
her signature are not only several new utility porcelains such
as the "Waves" service ensemble but also untold one-offs and
small series plus jewellery, accessories and murals. When ne-

gotiating "terra incognita", Sabine Wachs decorates her one-offs herself. She has been the Manufactory's Chief Designer since 2005. It was she who did the artistic groundwork for the Porcelain Museum façade. Ordering dimensional relations between the motifs in the various façade sections was key to her along with the play of harmonies and contrasts in the enlargements and also that between calligraphic and pictorial elements.

Gudrun Gaube (born 1961) has conceived many of the freshest patterns and is fain to be inspired by art nouveau or expressionist floral painting. Like her artist colleagues, she, too, fashions one-offs, including for the Pfeiffer celebrations in the year 2000 ("Hour Book of Nature"), the "Narrenfreiheit" exhibition held in Cologne in 2003 and the 2006 "ZWEIblicke" exhibition at the Meissen Gallery in Berlin. Upholding tradition without constraining modernity is a goal Gudrun Gaube sets herself. With her unconventional style she teases out the entire span of what can be achieved with porcelain. Individuality and specialist know-how inform her creativity.

Silvia Klöde (born 1956) is a graduate sculptress. In the course of her work she has created models for series production and studio porcelains. She studied Sculpture at the Fine Arts College in Dresden. She is notable for a series of medal designs for which she has also won prizes. She regularly works on engaging elements of interior design and is particularly given to figurative representation. Her female figurines are characterised by soft modelling, flowing lines and gently intercrescent body parts for the most part. They come across as universal symbols of inner strength, so self-contained and concise are they. Klöde is also partial to paro-

"Saphiens" service, created by Sabine Wachs with pattern by Volkmar Bretschneider and with handle plastic "Sisyphos" by Peter Strang, 1990

dying everyday foibles such as women's fashion follies. Her forms have recently started to become more abstract and, on occasions, angular.

Jörg Danielczyk (born 1952) studied at the Fine Arts College in Dresden. He was assistant to Peter Strang, his mentor for many years, from 1978 to 1983. Upon graduating, he became a leading artistic light at the Manufactory. He is particularly likely to put the most unusual artistic commissions to effect in porcelain. A large candelabra on the topic of hunting was completed in 2005, for instance. Some of his works are graphic art in porcelain — his sensitive formal vocabulary and sure stroke reveal how talented he is as a drawer. Porcelain had already profiled fashion, in the form of frock-coated cavaliers and their hoop-skirted ladies, back in the 18th century. Now it's the turn of fashion to profile porcelain. Danielczyk designed porcelain paillettes for fashion supremo Karl Lagerfeld and has since caught the bug. "Girls, Girls, Girls", a hit from the 1970s, is the name he gave an exhibition in Berlin in which he reveres the female sex and evokes a breath of haute couture in a manner reminiscent of Scheurich's porcelain graces. Danielczyk is

"Lady with Hat", created by Silvia Klöde, Sabine Wachs, 1992
Harlequin, created by Jörg Danielczyk, 2005

also Artistic Head of Whiteware Production and, in this function, is doing much for the "rebirth" of model porcelains.

Andreas Herten (born 1967) was long assistant and executor under Werner's instruction. He has been evolving his own creative potential since the 1990s, notably in the sphere of one-offs. Modernity and zeitgeist inform his work. He is the first artist to make extensive use of the airbrush technique when generating motifs, something that garnered him a personal exhibition in 2001 entitled "Aus der Luft gegriffen" (From Thin Air). This was so well-received that, in 2002, he gave a second presentation on the subject of "Airbrush and Painting on Porcelain" in Cologne. Spray guns have actually been used in porcelain manufacture since the end of the 19th century — in the painting of grounds, for instance — but Herten has trod virgin territory with them in the design of motifs on porcelain. His themes tend to inhabit the cusp between waking and dreaming. He is adept at playing with diffuse, mutating chromatic crossovers and with our imagination.

Olaf Fieber, Andreas Ehret and Christoph Ciesielki can be cited as representatives of the new generation, as can Horst Bretschneider and Manfred Fiksel. There are many others who deserve to be acknowledged here were it not for the constraints of space. Added to these are freelance visual artists who find it interesting to have done the odd job in this fine material. Some give up first go, others are smitten forever.

"Tell me what you eat and I will tell you who you are"

Table and banqueting culture has invariably been contextualised by the prevailing fashion, be it in music, literature, traditions or forms of behaviour. Fashions have come and gone since porcelain was invented, but births, weddings, receptions and balls continue to take place and the attendant festivities still have to be planned, organised and run with a good deal of imagination. These days, that stylish meal with the family or friends requires the right dining gear, i.e.

Bust "King", form and decoration by Olaf Fieber, 1997
Vase "Point of Vision", form and pattern by Andreas Herten in airbrush
technique, 2001 (unique copy, now private property)

a tablecloth, napkins, cutlery, glasses and, first and foremost, porcelain. The Manufactory has nominated "Waves" by Sabine Wachs as the "service of the millennial crossover" and it is also the service of the century, as "Grosser Ausschnitt" was before it. In line with a fine tradition, it is available in a smooth finish or with relief moulding. The waves of the relief gently ruffle the surfaces of cups and plates, rear up as they crash together on handles, and lap round the rather slender vessel forms. Decorated with either "Floral Tendrils", "Floral Enchantment", "Aqua", "Waterfowl", "Tulip and Poppy", "Woodland Flora with Insects", "Wild Poppy", "Cornflower" or a range of other patterns, this service will transform any dinner into a banquet.

At the pompous court festivities held in the 18th century table designs were a communicative highlight of what were known as "showpiece banquets". Later on, opulently adorned porcelain structures such as stylish centrepieces and thematically matching figurines took on this function. The Manufactory would like to return to this tradition, as its figurines were never meant for the showcase. There are occasions enough that merit laying out Meissen porcelain figures on a banquet table instead of − or in addition to − standard items such as flowers and candles. The Manufactory's huge repertoire certainly offers the wherewithal for so doing.

With this glance into the past and future of the Manufactory we have come to the end of our tour. But before leaving the Exhibition Hall there is one more extraordinary exhibit to admire. The most spectacular achievement of porcelain designer Ludwig Zepner is surely to have conceived an organ with porcelain pipes, which has been installed in the Exhibition Hall foyer. He has always addressed himself to the sound of porcelain with reference to the Börner team's bells. "...still always happy to travel such routes through unknown territory, he was destined to bring Börner's and Kaendler's futile attempts to a felicitous conclusion; even if it was only the acoustic problem that his famous predecessors had been unable to solve, this involved positioning the labium with such precision that the air column in the pipe is caused to vibrate intensely; that there were additionally other tasks to be tackled was comparatively irrelevant, as they concerned ceramic engineering — developing a ceramic form for the pipe, handling contraction of the porcelain paste during drying and firing, avoiding any deformation during firing ... He managed it."[15] Not on his own, of course. Such a venture

Concert in the Exhibition Hall with the world's first organ made of porcelain

could not have succeeded without co-involvement by experienced craftworkers at the Manufactory. The organ was built by Messrs Jehmlich of Dresden. It is enclosed by a splendid casing in solid pear. Christoph Ciesielki has lined the insides of the casing doors with Meissen porcelain tiles.

Postscript

A final word about Meissen wall art. Have you ever been to Dresden? Have you seen the Procession of Princes? That was the beginning. By the early 20th century, the Saxon Princes sgraffito applied by the painter Wilhelm Walther (1826–1913) had become so faded that, at the instigation of Julius Heintze, the scene was reproduced on around 25,000 porcelain tiles. Any number of public buildings, shops and restaurants have since been adorned with murals, façades and column cladding in porcelain. One gorgeous example from the most recent past is a 90-square-metre wall mosaic entitled "Saxony's loveliest palaces, castles and gardens" that was produced for the concourse at Dresden Neustadt railway station to a design by Heinz Werner and Horst Bretschneider. Over 900 such schemes have been completed since 1958 and their number is rising steadily. Examples are also on display in the Porcelain Museum café, in the foyers and by the stairs. Some 20 painters and technical operatives work in a dedicated "Artistic Mural" department. Their next mural in Meissen Porcelain® could be for you!

"Is Meissen Porcelain® modern?" was the question we began by posing. Why talk of Vieux Saxe or Old-Style Meissen if Meissen Porcelain® is so timeless? The answer is that old and new are interdependent at the Manufactory, which is what we are all about. Forms and models, formulae and

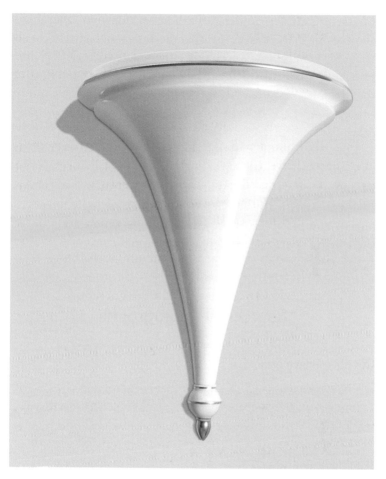

Mural painting with bracket, by Sabine Wachs, 2007

skills have come down through the centuries. Our artisans are constantly compelled to gauge themselves against what is on show in the Exhibition Hall, to retrace the inspiration of their predecessors and to shoulder fresh challenges.

Meissen®'s understanding of tradition does not, therefore, confine itself to preserving specific forms of artistic excellence for generations and having the entire historical repertoire at its fingertips. It has always additionally been part of the Meissen® tradition to ongoingly add to the legacy and in this way meet the demand for premium contemporary porcelain.

Thus the question as to whether Meissen Porcelain® is modern does not present itself. As it has always done, the Manufactory strives to create artistic and utility porcelains that are stylistically formative, reflective of their age, balanced, complete, precious and classic – which adds up to their being timeless and hence forever modern.

Sources of Photographs

Endnotes

1 Sales staff card index for the trade. VEB Staatliche Porzellan Manufaktur Meissen-DDR, 1986, card 87.

2 Jürgen Schärer: Auf den Punkt gebracht. Porzellane aus Meissen Max Adolf Pfeiffer zu Ehren. Published by Staatliche Porzellan-Manufaktur Meissen 2000, p. 73

3 Karl Berling: Das Meissener Porzellan und seine Geschichte. Leipzig, 1900.

4 Dr Hannes Walter: Interview entitled "Zur Erfindung des europäischen Hartporzellans" in Keramischer Rundblick, 2006, p. 429.

5 Adolf Brüning: Porzellan. Manuals of the Royal Museums in Berlin, Arts and Crafts Museum; revised by L. Schnorr v. Carolsfeld, Berlin, 1914.

6 Hans Sonntag: Die Botschaft des Drachen. Ostasiatische Glückssymbole auf Meissener Porzellan. Leipzig, 1993.

7 Karl Berling: Festschrift zur 200jährigen Jubelfeier der ältesten europäischen Porzellanmanufaktur Meißen 1910. Leipzig, 1911, pp. 29/30.

8 Lutz Miedtank: "Zwiebelmuster". Zur 300jährigen Geschichte des Dekors auf Porzellan, Fayence und Steingut. Leipzig, 1991, p. 35.

9 Ibid., pp 39/40.

10 Berling, as note 3.

11 Dresdner Presse dated 25 June 1873, Year 2, No. 175.

12 Max Adolf Pfeiffer: Das Wesen des Porzellans (1923) as cited in: Bröhan 1977, Vol. II, Part 2, p. 299.

13 Reports issued by Staatliche Porzellan-Manufaktur Meissen, 1919, Max Adolf Pfeiffer, Works Archive No. 1230, pp. 12 f.

14 Meissener Konturen 1960–1990. Catalogue for the exhibition of the same name held in 1992. Leipzig, 1991, p. 18.

15 Schärer, as Note 4.

Chronological Table

1701	Johann Friedrich Böttger imprisoned in Saxony.
1704	Böttger works with Ehrenfried Walter von Tschirnhaus.
1705/6	Böttger toils with Freiberg miners in Albrechtsburg Castle.
1706	Böttger is taken to Königstein fortress to prevent him falling into the hands of Swedish King Charles XII.
1707	In a newly set-up laboratory within the Jungfernbastei fortification in Dresden, Tschirnhaus oversees the work of Böttger and the Freiberg mining and smelting experts.
1707/8	Böttger invents red stoneware.
1709	Böttger announces the invention of white porcelain in a "memorandum" to Augustus the Strong, King of Poland and Prince-Elector of Saxony, on 28 March.
1710	A patent published by Augustus the Strong proclaims the formation of the porcelain manufactory in four languages (Latin, German, French and Dutch).
	Brown stoneware is presented for the first time at the Leipzig Fair.
	Albrechtsburg Castle in Meißen becomes the first production site on 6 June.
	Böttger is appointed the first administrator on 29 December.
1713	White porcelain is shown for the first time at the Leipzig Easter Fair.
1714	Böttger regains his freedom on 19 April.
1719	Böttger dies on 13 March at the age of 37.
1720	The painter and chemist Johann Gregorius Höroldt joins the Manufactory.
1723	The crossed electoral swords are introduced as an official mark. Höroldt becomes Painter to the Court.
1731	Augustus the Strong assumes overall control of the Manufactory.
	On 22 June, Johann Joachim Kaendler is called to Meißen as Chief Modeller.

	The royal court orders 132 large-format animals and 120 birds for the Japanese Palace in Dresden.
1733	Kaendler takes over Kirchner's post as Chief Modeller upon the latter leaving in February.
	Augustus the Strong dies on 1 February. His son and successor, at once Prince-Elector Frederick Augustus II of Saxony and King Augustus III of Poland, hands overall control to his first minister, Count Brühl.
1737	Kaendler and Eberlein begin designing the Swan Service for Count Brühl.
1739	Count Brühl becomes Overall Director in Meissen. Blue Onion is launched together with a new glaze that enhances the effect of blue-and-white painting.
1740	Kaendler becomes Head of the moulders', modellers' and throwers' workshops.
1756	Seven Years' War begins and production temporarily ceases.
1774	Overall control of the Manufactory is assumed by Count Marcolini.
1775	With the deaths of Höroldt (26 January) and Kaendler (18 May), two titans of European porcelain pass on.
1810	Work at Albrechtsburg Castle comes to a halt. The Manufactory has just 435 employees on its books. The first centenary of its formation is overshadowed by fraught circumstances.
1814	Heinrich Gottlob Kühn assumes technical control and oversees countless innovations.
1817	Johann Samuel Arnhold designs the "Full Green Vineleaf Garland" pattern.
1828	The first lithophanes are made at the Manufactory. Adrian Ludwig Richter is appointed Chief Drawer at the Drawing School.
1830	Kühn develops burnished gold, a gilt decoration that does not require polishing once fired.
1849	Kühn is appointed Manufactory Director and Mining Counsellor. Ernst August Leuteritz becomes supervisor of the design department.

1853	First steam engine operated by the Meissen Porcelain Manufactory at Albrechtsburg Castle.
1861	Foundation stone laid on 28 May for new premises in the Triebisch Valley area of Meißen.
1862	The Manufactory records considerable commercial successes at the third international exposition in London.
1863/65	Porcelain Manufactory moves to new premises in the Triebisch Valley.
1867	The Manufactory wins a top prize at the fourth international exposition in Paris.
1885	At the international exposition in Antwerp, the Manufactory wins top prize for its overall display.
1893	Meissen® presents over 1,000 items at the international exposition in Chicago including two large-size mirrors, a jewellery cabinet by Sturm, a crater vase with the Alexandrian Procession painted in gold and platinum, pâte-sur-pâte works and a wide range in high-fire colours.
1900	At the Paris international exposition, Meissen® presents traditional material alongside novelties such as the "Crocus" déjeuner by Konrad Hentschel and porcelains with crystal glazes.
1903	The Manufactory buys drafts by Richard Riemerschmid and Henry van de Velde. Erich Hösel is appointed Design Supervisor.
1907	Completion of the 101.9-metre Procession of Princes, painted on 25,000 porcelain tiles, on the outer wall of the royal stables at Dresden Castle.
1910	The Manufactory celebrates the bicentenary of its formation on 6 June with 1,400 staff and 700 guests.
1916	Inauguration of the Exhibition Hall.
1918	The Manufactory is renamed Meissen State Porcelain Manufactory. Max Adolf Pfeiffer takes on the directorship and calls artists of note to the Manufactory, amongst them Paul Scheurich, Max Esser, Gerhard Marcks and Ernst Barlach.
1926	Pfeiffer is appointed Director General in December.

1929	On the occasion of Meißen's millennial celebrations, Emil Paul Börner designs the city's Church of St. Nicholas as a memorial for the dead of the First World War. The first set of playable porcelain bells, also attributed to Börner, is installed in Meißen's Church of our Lady.
1930	Börner becomes Artistic Director.
1933	Following the seizure of power by the Nazis, Pfeiffer is dismissed. The number of employees falls to 612.
1937	Works by Paul Scheurich and Max Esser win top prizes at the international exposition in Paris.
1944	Contents of Exhibition Hall placed in cellars of Albrechtsburg Castle for safekeeping.
1945	Manufactory buildings hit by artillery fire in the course of military action in the Meißen area. Production ceases. Manufactory becomes Soviet joint-stock company.
1950	The enterprise is renamed the People's Own Meissen State Porcelain Manufactory on 23 June.
1959	Return to the Manufactory of items from the Exhibition Hall that had been taken to the Soviet Union.
1960	Festive 250th anniversary celebrations on 6 June at Albrechtsburg Castle. For the first time since the Second World War, porcelain can again be shown in the Exhibition Hall. Ludwig Zepner, Peter Strang and Heinz Werner form the "Artistic Development Collective".
1969	Prof. Dr.-Ing. Karl Petermann assumes the company's directorship, a post he holds until 1983. He oversees the commencement of revamping and extending the Manufactory.
1970	The foundation stone for a new firing house is laid on 8 May.
1973	Ludwig Zepner develops the forms for the "Grosser Ausschnitt" service.
1982	Festivities and international scientific symposium on the tercentenary of the birth of Johann Friedrich Böttger. "Oldest and Newest from Meissen" exhibition held in the Albertinum in Dresden.

1989	250th anniversary of "Meissen Blue Onion".
1990	Company name reverts to "Meissen State Porcelain Manufactory".
1991	The Manufactory passes wholly into the property of the State of Saxony on 6 June. Ceremony to mark the 75th anniversary of the Exhibition Hall.
1992	A new generation of artists show off their work at the "Von Wegen" exhibition held at Albrechtsburg Castle in Meißen.
1992	Exhibition Hall makeover, 175th anniversary of "Full Green Vineleaf Garland".
1995	Ceremony and special exhibition to mark the 50th anniversary of the death of Paul Scheurich.
1996	Jubilee celebrations and special exhibitions in Dresden and Meißen to mark the tercentenary of the birth of Johann Gregorius Höroldt.
2000	Appreciation of the work done by Max Adolf Pfeiffer for the Meissen Manufactory on the occasion of the 125th anniversary of his birth. The "Waves" service by Sabine Wachs is unveiled.
2005	Handover of the extended Porcelain Museum with its newly designed façade, comprising a mural in porcelain, glass and concrete 35 metres long and 9 metres high, on which the artist Sabine Wachs "narrates" the history of the Porcelain Manufactory.
2006	Events and exhibitions on the tercentenary of the birth of Johann Joachim Kaendler.